The Journey of Hindi Language Journalism in India

<h1 style="text-align:center">Studies in Journalism</h1>

The Studies in Journalism series will comprise monographs, edited volumes and textbooks on various aspects of the academic discipline of journalism and mass communication. The volumes in this series have been envisaged as interactive guides on reporting, coverage and opinion pieces. Ranging from the theoretically-bent to the empirically-argued, the books will draw cases from across the spectrum of practices, trends and visions within the journalistic profession in this part of the world. This series is aimed at students and teachers of journalism, journalists, freelance writers and media professionals.

Series Editor
Nalini Rajan, *Professor, Asian College of Journalism, Chennai.*

The Journey of Hindi Language Journalism in India

From Raj to Swaraj and Beyond

MRINAL PANDE

Orient BlackSwan

THE JOURNEY OF HINDI LANGUAGE JOURNALISM IN INDIA: FROM RAJ TO SWARAJ AND BEYOND

ORIENT BLACKSWAN PRIVATE LIMITED

Registered Office
3-6-752 Himayatnagar, Hyderabad 500 029 (Telangana), INDIA
e-mail: centraloffice@orientblackswan.com

Other Offices
Bengaluru, Chennai, Guwahati, Hyderabad, Kolkata,
Mumbai, New Delhi, Noida, Patna

© Orient Blackswan Private Limited 2022
First published by Orient Blackswan Pvt. Ltd. 2022
Paperback edition 2024

ISBN 978-93-5442-820-3

Typeset in Goudy Old Style 11/13
by Jojy Philip, New Delhi 110 015

Printed in India at
Shree Maitrey Printech Pvt. Ltd., Noida

Published by
Orient Blackswan Private Limited
3-6-752 Himayatnagar, Hyderabad 500 029
Telangana, India
e-mail: info@orientblackswan.com

038571

Contents

List of Tables

List of Abbreviations

ABC	Audit Bureau of Circulations
AFP	Agence France-Presse
AIR	All India Radio
ANI	Asian News International
AP	Associated Press
ASCI	Administrative Staff College of India
BBC	British Broadcasting Corporation
BIMARU	Bihar, Madhya Pradesh, Rajasthan and Uttar Pradesh
BJP	Bharatiya Janata Party
BOC	Bureau of Outreach and Communication
DAVP	Directorate of Advertising and Visual Publicity
DMK	Dravida Munnetra Kazhagam
DTH	direct-to-home
ECI	Election Commission of India
EOT	Embedded OpenType (font file format)
ERNET	Education and Research Network
FDI	foreign direct investment
FIR	First Information Report
GST	Goods and Services Tax
IAMAI	Internet and Mobile Association of India
IANS	Indo-Asian News Service

IIT	Indian Institute of Technology
IPO	Initial Public Offering
IRS	Indian Readership Survey
IT	information technology
IWPC	Indian Women's Press Club
MGNREGA	Mahatma Gandhi National Rural Employment Guarantee Act, 2005
MOM	Media Ownership Monitor
MRUC	Media Research Users Council
NDA	National Democratic Alliance
NGO	non-governmental organisation
NIC	National Informatics Centre
NICNET	NIC Network
NRS	National Readership Survey
NWMI	Network of Women in Media, India
OBC	Other Backward Class
PCI	Press Council of India
PMO	Prime Minister's Office
PTI	Press Trust of India
RPA	Representation of the People Act, 1951
RTI	Right to Information Act, 2005
SAP	Systems, Applications, Products in Data Processing
TRAI	Telecom Regulatory Authority of India
UNDP	United Nations Development Programme
UNESCO	United Nations Educational, Scientific and Cultural Organisation
UNI	United News of India
UP	Uttar Pradesh
VSNL	Videsh Sanchar Seva Nigam Ltd.

Introduction

The basic idea for writing this book had long been dormant within me. The final nudge came from the publisher. As I began working on the book, the question arose: Where should one begin? Should one focus on internet-led changes in content and format, and the rising revenue potential of new media in Hindi? But that makes no sense without first introducing readers to the gradual development of Hindi journalism since the beginning of the twentieth century: the growth and changes within India and its media, its tryst with destiny, the actual events, led by men and women who shaped the world of India's politics and gave us a Constitution that fostered freedom of expression. Then, there is another sub-plot: the managers and marketing staff who worked day and night, often in the worst possible conditions, to finally create a vast market for Hindi media, carrying political debates and ideologies into the remotest corners of the Hindi heartland. All of them must be placed within the Hindi media story. They are the ones who actually helped restore and nurture individual self-esteem and an overarching need for human freedoms in a country that had no living memory of a democratic State.

True, today there are many regional biases against the Hindi language, especially in the non-Hindi speaking areas. They stem not from a dislike for the language, but from Hindi's perceived proximity to political leaders and prime ministers, most of whom have belonged to the Hindi heartland. Several times, powerful political leaders, keen to play up to their vote-banks in the northern plains, have unfairly pushed for Hindi to be India's sole official language. Then, there are the upwardly-mobile, urban middle classes, convinced of the superiority of the English language over all of India's vernaculars. Their representatives in the bureaucracy, the academy and the media houses describe the English-language media as the 'national media', while vernacular media to them remains regional, despite its far bigger footprint and impact. Hindi is the largest spoken language because it is mother tongue to almost a dozen northern states. The unfettered demographic growth and expansion of literacy in the Hindi heartland expanded the market for Hindi newspapers, even though literacy levels and incomes in the north have been much lower than those in the southern states. All these together created a mindset that overlooked the full commercial and political power of Hindi media for many decades after Independence. This impacted the quality of Hindi publications, which were seldom noticed, quoted or awarded technical and human resources on par with the English media by the owners of multi-language publications, the publicity departments of various governments, and the advertising and marketing agencies.

So what tripped the lock for Hindi?

All books about revolutionary change should begin with a psychological chapter, says the Polish journalist Ryszard Kapuściński (1985), that shows exactly when and how a harassed, terrified crowd stops being terrified and stands up for itself. For the Hindi media, that moment came after the government-imposed, two-year Emergency (of 1975–77) was lifted. Around the early 1980s, many young Hindi writers and journalists, who had felt the foetid breath of censorship on their skin between 1975 and 1977, chose to quit various other jobs to enter Hindi journalism. I was one of them. I joined a Hindi-language news agency around 1981, when no one of any public standing—political leaders, bureaucrats, even most revolutionary writers of tracts against the Emergency in English—would waste their time or attention on journalists from some obscure Hindi news agency they had never heard of. Even the agency journalists, I discovered, had low self-esteem. The day I reported for work, the head of the agency asked me bluntly, 'What possessed you to quit a good job and join this agency?' So much for encouraging beginnings.

Then, I was introduced to my fellow workers—a sea of male employees of various ages. I saw no females. All my fellow workers, without exception, at some point or another, would wonder aloud what I thought I was doing at Samachar Bharati, after dumping a perfectly decent job of teaching English literature to undergraduates at one of the best colleges in Delhi University. Under such a barrage of questions, it was some time before I found my real voice and located my own areas of interest. Gradually, a sort of peace descended upon us. We were all equally ill-paid and ill-equipped, weren't we? So we chose to plod bravely on and look out for each other.

Other discoveries followed: the services of Hindi news agencies were mostly engaged by Hindi dailies, who grabbed the content transmitted to them regularly, but seldom paid their bills on time, if at all. The VIPs in Delhi would not meet or even answer phone calls from a mere representative from a Hindi news agency. But they were readily available to our English-language counterparts. Hindi journalists, I was advised, should forget about cultivating 'sources' among the ranks of important bureaucrats and corporates. They had no interest in the vernacular media. We would, we were told, be better off cultivating as sources senior clerks, peons and drivers, who were privy to much secret conversation. If all else failed, we translated furiously from news stories that the sister English daily would share with us.

One of my friends, the daughter of Mukut Bihari Verma, the first editor (1941–63) of *Hindustan Dainik* (a major Hindi daily of the Hindustan Times group), shared an article by her late father (published posthumously in *Lokraj Varshiki*, 1977). It makes no bones about how much his Hindi daily depended on the English daily, *Hindustan Times*, then edited by Mahatma Gandhi's son, Devdas Gandhi. To save costs, he writes, the Hindi daily was expected to pick and translate most of its articles (ready, edited, and inclusive of the headlines), handed to them by the English daily before being sent to press. For several years after Independence, they had a small staff and no foreign or even outstation correspondents, nor regular correspondents for covering sessions of the newly formed Houses of Parliament. For rural reporting, they used the social workers working among farmers in rural areas. They drew their exclusivity from the fact that they would report Mahatma Gandhi's or other leaders' important Hindi speeches verbatim. Few people today know that when the British government jailed Devdas Gandhi and the publisher, Devidas, Verma was also incarcerated. He has high praise for Devdas Gandhi, who, he writes, readily shared news and also used his clout to get the stubborn Parliament secretariat to issue a pass for the correspondent of the house Hindi daily as well.

But in the heady, post-Emergency 1980s, after the media's frozen freedoms were restored, the greatest joy my generation of Hindi journalists experienced came from being polyphone gatherers of all sorts of news and information. The literary and cultural scene that prevailed lent us an inclusive Hindi, re-energised by various regional dialects: Braj, Awadhi, Purabiya, Kumaoni. This variously flavoured Hindi became the most apt vehicle for not just political stories about our democracy, but a whole new climate that voiced the innermost feelings of the Hindi heartland—the myths and legends, gossip from its parliament, secretariats, streets and lanes—the thousand elements of reality that were forming Indian democracy. The English papers often published such stories in 600 words in a side column. But we, the Hindi journalists, that had the ear of both rural and urban readers, the blue-collar workers and the farmers, were free to improvise. We began taking wild liberties with the format for describing the stories that flew out of the Kumbh Mela, train accidents in far-off towns, brides murdered for dowry, female dacoits taking revenge on upper-caste rapists after lining them up and shooting them like ducks in a row. We managed to draw a whole new readership to Hindi periodicals: dailies, weeklies, fortnightlies, quarterlies and annuals. Our young audiences were as news-hungry, politically aware and unafraid as us. And what is more, we saw their numbers growing each year beyond our wildest dreams.

Despite the enormous financial clout and socio-political advantages it had, English-language journalism of those years seemed far more traditional and lily-livered to us. What is more, we were networking with other languages and making Hindi a major catchment area for the best works from all vernaculars: S. L. Bhyrappa, Sarat Chandra Chattopadhyay, K. M. Munshi, Bibhutibhushan Bandyopadhyay, Amrita Pritam, Padma Sachdev, U. R. Ananthamurthy, Badal Sarkar, Girish Karnad and Prasanna, were all available in Hindi translations as soon as they were published in their native tongues. Magazines serialised their works and introduced the writers to appreciative audiences and theatre buffs in the Hindi belt. In contrast, the Indo-Anglian writers mostly seemed to be looking over their shoulders to see if their counterparts in the West were appreciative or not. Behind the closed doors of media organisations, however, English reigned as the dominant language of all power discourse. And despite their comparatively small readership, the English dailies were feted and admired as the voice of the nation, while Hindi dailies, with their readership stretching over 11 of the most populous states in the north, were seen as 'regional'.

But one must confess, it was irritating when social perceptions affected our professional access to news. At important press conferences held in the capital city of New Delhi, for example, a vernacular journalist had to risk being called a 'troublemaker' and shout to be noticed. The questions and answers in any important government–media exchange following major international meets or the annual Union budget were nearly always between males and in English. In addition to this, a rare female, who defied odds and rose to be editor, had to face frequent confrontations with misogyny and insubordination by her own senior male staff.

Then, there was the universe of printing presses. As night descended and the machines began rolling out the next day's news, the usual macho work-rhythms became laced with sweat, alcohol, grease-paint and ink fumes. But these simple men in greasy overalls, I was moved to discover, actually read each page of the Hindi dailies and periodicals they helped print each night. Some of them were fans of my mother's fiction, serialised in the house weeklies, and said they avidly awaited each new segment. They were extra kind and accommodating to their favourite writer's child, and once they recognised honest hard work and integrity, borders between boss and subordinate dissolved totally. They would occasionally stride into my cabin after a significant event and suggest that 'down below' they were saying I should write a signed editorial: 'Madam *ji, aaj tau hamaare liye ek dhamaakedaar* signed front-page editorial *kerna hee hoga*' (Madam, today you must write a truly explosive signed, front-page editorial for our sakes!). Their innate, native sense of justice and care for the Hindi publications kept me going through some very painful years.

A job in Hindi media was well worth the trouble in many other ways as well. In researching and interacting with all kinds of people, organisations and political functionaries in the public spaces created by Hindi, one interacted with a whole thriving world of regional publications. In contrast to the owners/publishers of multi-edition dailies and periodicals in both English and Hindi from Delhi or Mumbai, the owners/publishers in regional capitals usually treated their Hindi publications and their staff with greater deference, primarily because these owners themselves spoke and read Hindi, as did the regional political satraps. By the second half of the 1980s, regional owners had begun investing well and wisely in the latest and best technology on offer, and employed professional designers to create perfect grids for their publications. The salaries they paid may have been smaller, but in the Hindi heartland, Hindi dailies and news magazines had become opinion creators and were avidly followed by the general public as well as by top politicians and bureaucrats.

Due to the socio-political culture of the Hindi belt, nearly all these publications remained upper caste-centric and female deficient. There were no women editors in Hindi for a long time, despite the effects of the first ever national report on the status of women (Committee on the Status of Women in India 1974) and another one on women workers in the unorganised sector (*Shramshakti* 1988), that created major ripples among policymakers. Within provincial newsrooms, traditional ideas about women's work and status within society have taken a longer time to change. However, the all-male teams chosen for editorial work had a good mix of seasoned hands and upwardly mobile, young graduates, far more enthusiastic, at home with and confident of their Hindi papers' reach and influence. They needed some, but not too much, convincing about the need to make newsrooms and their publications more inclusive. And also, would they please use a more colloquial Hindi, laced with dialects?

In the 1980s and 1990s, coalitional governments became routine and the new incumbents that swam up the political waters in state capitals were fluent in Hindi and used it not only at electoral rallies, but also within Parliament as a badge of identity. During my three-year stay in Bhopal, the capital of the then vast and undivided Madhya Pradesh, I woke up to a range of fast-growing, charismatic regional Hindi dailies: *Nai Dunia* of Indore, *Aaj* of Varanasi, *Swatantra Bharat* of Lucknow and *Dainik Pradip* of Patna. It was in Bhopal that I became an avid reader of the dynamic and till then hugely underrated

Indore-based publication, *Nai Dunia* (founded in 1954). Rajendra Mathur, the then editor of *Nai Dunia* (and later of the Times Group's multi-edition daily, *Navbharat Times*, in New Delhi), had also arrived on the Hindi scene with a master's degree in English literature. He had begun working as a cub reporter for *Nai Dunia* while still in college, encouraged by its wonderfully well-informed and astute editor, Rahul Barpute, who had talent-spotted him early. Mathur took over the paper after his mentor and editor, Barpute, retired. It was my long association with Mathur that disabused me forever of many myths about Hindi journalism, one being that all Hindi journalists are at heart monolingual, provincial dolts who do not read much in other languages, let alone follow major international developments intelligently.

I realised that provincial journalists like Mathur came in with rich educational backgrounds and were sharp connoisseurs of various traditional art forms. Barpute of *Nai Dunia*, for example, was an agricultural scientist by training and also one of the closest friends of Kumar Gandharva, the great Hindustani musician. Senior editor, Prabhash Joshi, wrote equally brilliantly on politics and cricket. Then there was the satirist-playwright, Sharad Joshi, who wrote a daily column for *Nai Dunia* and later, *Navbharat Times* (founded in 1950). 'I said to myself, if Art Buchwald can, why can't Sharad?' said Mathur. Sharad Joshi was later to become an early celebrity script-writer for Doordarshan serials like *Yeh jo hai zindagi*.

These Hindi journalists were a rare bunch of restless, reckless, risk-takers, firmly rooted in their language. A similar soul was Ashok Agrawal of *Swatantra Bharat* in Lucknow, sharp of mind as a journalist, and friend and mentor to various academics, musicians and Hindi writers. In Rajasthan, there was Karpoor Chand 'Kulish', founder-editor of *Rajasthan Patrika* (founded in 1956). The man was a local institution, a Sanskrit scholar and authority on the Vedas. In the west, Lala Jagat Narayan's popular *Punjab Kesari*, headquartered in Jalandhar, was flourishing, as also its Urdu counterpart, *Ajit. Punjab Kesari* was named after the Punjab celebrity leader, Lala Lajpat Rai, who had first launched it in 1929. Narayan relaunched it in 1966, and by the late 1970s, it had already overtaken the Delhi-based Hindi dailies of the Times and Hindustan Times groups. All these owners and their editors had taken the pulse of the region and did not hesitate to use the locally spoken version of Hindi, instead of the formal, academic one. They were sure of their professional power and confident of their clout.

The provincial owners of Hindi newspapers that I met in the 1980s and 1990s were not merely shrewd businessmen ready to exploit the swiftly widening public sphere created for news in Hindi. More often than not, they were also risk-takers, driven as much by the desire to earn more, as by a genuine thirst for knowledge gathered and transmitted formally to the public of their state in a clear, colloquial Hindi. One prime example was Seth Labhchand Chhajlani of *Nai Dunia*, who had been the driving force behind the pre-Independence Praja Mandal movement in the erstwhile Holkar state. He attracted bright young iconoclasts like Barpute to his paper like a magnet with iron filings. Another was the Chennai-based, spunky Marwari, Ramnath Goenka, a Bihar-born trader turned media empire builder, whose Hindi daily, *Jansatta*, was launched in Delhi and edited for over a decade by Prabhash Joshi. Joshi, with whom I frequently and happily agreed or disagreed with over professional matters at the Editors' Guild, was an awesome iconoclast who bravely defied communalism and Hindutva ideologues, and led the crusade against the phenomenon of 'paid news' in his last years.

Like floods causing devastation but also enriching the land by depositing layers of rich alluvial soil, the receding Emergency waters left a fertile field behind for Hindi-language media. The active promotion of investigative reporting, and greater and more intense interaction between the media and politicians they had helped promoted a growth in the reading public across the Hindi belt. The relaxed rules for importing new machinery and newsprint also helped owners to create better infrastructure for printing and marketing. But by and by, the same opportunities came to be used as a tool by many ambitious media barons to help individual politicians' agendas and promote specific party ideologies. At the same time, publicising grievances or defying power created powerful enemies for journalists, who were retrenched by owners under pressure, or threatened or physically attacked. There were several instances of Hindi editors quietly being replaced by the proprietors at the behest of politicians or corporates whom they had offended by exposing some wrongdoing or another.

Despite their small budgets, scores of major Hindi dailies had editors who were also eminent writers of Hindi prose and poetry. As journalism expanded the public space for Hindi, all major publishing houses and also the government-controlled All India Radio (AIR) and Doordarshan, began enrolling well-known Hindi writers. By the late 1980s, several stalwarts of Hindi that I had grown up reading were multitasking within print, radio and later, in TV. These gifted multitaskers and desperados from small backwater towns kept alive their familial ties with the rural backwaters, various dialects and also Urdu. They used their knowledge to further hone and enrich Hindi journalism as they talked to audiences who avoided the starchy, Sanskrit-laden Hindi of AIR news bulletins and Hindi's literary critics. Back in Delhi, the major publishing houses paid their editorial staff in Hindi somewhat better than their regional rivals, but much less than they paid the editors of their counterparts in English dailies. The atmosphere at the workplace too was far more conducive to bold experimentation in the regional dailies headquartered in the Hindi states, away from Delhi.

By the 1990s, the owners of most major newspapers were a little too well-integrated with the machinery of the State. India's political parties and the bureaucracy had also grudgingly accepted the vast political potential of India's Hindi heartland. And all wished to use the vibrant public sphere Hindi media had crafted to communicate with the masses and win elections. The 1990s were a period of vast growth for Hindi, not only in the Hindi belt, but also in other states where diasporic *bhaiyas* (brothers) from Uttar Pradesh (UP) and Bihar had settled as the economy boomed. The stoutly pro-Bangla, pro-English Ananda Bazar Group of Calcutta began publishing a Hindi news weekly, *Ravivar*, partly to mop up the considerable readership that existed in the eastern region, and also to snatch readers away from the Times Group's wildly popular Hindi weekly, *Dharmyug*, and the Hindustan Times group's almost as popular *Saptahik Hindustan*. Chapters 1–4 in this book describe the changes, and the socio-economic policies that brought this about, sequentially and in some detail.

Over the years, the localisation of news and the rise of a reading habit in the Hindi belt also began to exact, subtly at first and then openly, a price from Hindi journalism. The earliest threats came from the State. Several Hindi media barons had, by then, been nominated to the Upper House of Parliament. This had twin benefits: first, it ensured a fire cover for their other businesses, and second, it guaranteed positive coverage for the political party that nominated them. Younger Hindi journalists spoke in hushed tones of the great clout that some of the senior Hindi hands had come to have; who among them enjoyed special proximity to the media advisor to the prime minister or the finance minister, and had in turn gained swift upward mobility at the workplace. Some capitalists turned newspaper owners and brought out Hindi publications. Several that already had Hindi dailies began to release regional editions and also English dailies. The latter were largely aimed at prestige and connectivity with the Lutyens' Delhi power packs for their owners, and also at mopping up advertisements for upmarket goods available only to English dailies.

Private TV news channels' advent into the market around 1995 began a churning in the mediascape that the established Hindi dailies eyed with suspicion. As a country with a greater predilection for oral transmission of news, TV posed a threat. But TV news cost money, so unless owners also had an entertainment channel to cross-subsidise the news channel, the venture was bound to close sooner rather than later. The dailies heaved a sigh of relief after they realised that it would be some time before TV maximised its profits.

Between 1997 and 2001, I briefly stepped into the newly expanding field of TV news as a Hindi anchor-cum-editor, first into a private channel, and later into India's public broadcaster, Doordarshan. TV news was then in its nascent stage, but it was fast becoming obvious that even in the world of television, Hindi and the vernaculars would always command more eyeballs than English. But the marketing and management of TV remained Anglocentric for another decade. In both public and private TV news channels I encountered, apart from the usual language-based hierarchies, the policymaking groups, and input and output desks were invariably headed by English-speaking owners/managers, journalists and anchors. Doordarshan revealed clear, gender-based discrimination aimed only at senior women journalists, not their male counterparts. With no data to back it up, the male reasoning was that 'modern' Indian viewers preferred young and nubile female anchors as presenters of news on TV, preferably in Western attire. That grey hair in men lent a certain gravitas, but greying female anchors must hang up their gloves.

By this time, I had realised that the myths about selfless 'service' rendered to Mother Hindi by *Hindi-wallahs* (people whose first language is Hindi) who accepted being paid less than their English counterparts, and the audiences' rejection of ageing female news anchors, were elaborate hoaxes. They kept the vernacular media and seasoned female journalists off the fat of the media land. If these were the rules of the game, I felt, we must not accept genteel poverty and remain Gandhian nationalists, but use our considerable experience to demand respect, better salaries and working conditions. In 1995, cutting across linguistic and regional boundaries, 17 of us senior women journalists founded the Indian Women's Press Club (IWPC). This meant that India's women journalists had come to matter and were ready to defy the boundaries that male journalists we had interacted with over the years, and still fraternised with, had rarely had to jostle with. To their credit, once senior male journalists accepted our credentials, they had our back at all times. Multitasking constantly at work and at home, most of us, unlike males, were brought up to listen and to expect a certain civility when we spoke. Our long years in the media seeded the media space with this ethos. It may still take longer to create a level playing field for both English and Hindi, males and females, Dalits and non-Dalits. But one must record here, especially for young millennials, that respected media bodies like the Press Club, the Editors' Guild and the Media Foundation of India, have not just helped the IWPC in our rough initial years, but also happily accepted the presence of women journalists in senior positions. All this, and the arrival of technology that helped demolish pyramidal hierarchies within the papers to create more horizontal and less graded newsrooms, has ushered in many healthy changes.

Today, Hindi is a huge part of the mediascape in India, and watching new technology change the power balance in newsrooms and in the marketplace is an almost surreal experience for my generation. All of a sudden, communication in colloquial Hindi is needed all over. The lawmakers need it, the law enforcers need it, the markets need it. And all the new media stars, not just the ones in Bollywood but even those handling streaming platforms, want

Hindi subtitles, no matter what their engagement with Hindi in their personal lives is. The game has changed almost overnight.

By the year 2009, when I left the Hindustan Times group where I was group editor for Hindi, a new generation of owners was gradually emerging in all major publishing houses. By the first decade of the new century, market-savvy managers had started a process of reformatting and repositioning the Hindi dailies, which they realised were going to be the future flagship publications. The young hands in Hindi were amazingly fast in learning to handle the new technology. Gradually, salaries began to improve, as also the look and feel of all major Hindi dailies in the market. This, and the push in sales, the coffee machines and open-plan offices with see-through glass partitions, have now replaced the older silos between the Hindi and English editorials. They have also abolished many old hierarchies and created a more women-friendly work-space for the rising number of new female staff. The mysterious, closed-door editorial spaces and old-style editorial work-flow systems that had created many secret opportunities for sexual harassment disappeared, even though old-style gender-baiting or Hindi vs. English rivalries occasionally raise their ugly heads.

In the second decade of the twenty-first century, the major Hindi dailies, like *Jagran*, *Bhaskar* and *Hindustan*, aggressively supported by managerial teams, began to cannibalise regional dailies by swiftly launching dozens of regional editions one after another. *Dainik Jagran*, already a success in UP and Delhi, launched an edition in Patna, followed by *Dainik Bhaskar*, another mega Hindi daily. Today, each of the two top dailies, *Dainik Jagran* and *Dainik Bhaskar*, has over 50 regional editions, printed at over three dozen locations. The regional editions have also introduced a page for each district, compiled mostly by freelancers (who also double up as marketing agents selling space for the district pages) and dispatched to the nearest print centre digitally.

Meanwhile, with the arrival of the internet and digitised news platforms, insecurities are growing among the older, seasoned media hands. Up until 1998, it was a government monopoly and Videsh Sanchar Seva Nigam Ltd. (VSNL) was the main service provider. After it was privatised, the subscriber base exploded. The dot-com phase had already begun around 1993, when Hindi websites like *Gofor*

India, *Gappu* and *Newspaperonline* surfaced. But most of these, like the earliest Hindi newspapers of the nineteenth century, shut down soon for lack of professional handling of news content. Around 2003, all major Hindi dailies and independent news channels launched their own e-papers and websites. The British Broadcasting Corporation (BBC) also launched its popular website in Hindi. Today, *Aaj Tak News*, *Dainik Bhaskar*, *Rajasthan Patrika*, *Navbharat Times*, *Web Dunia*, *IBN Khabar* are among the most read digital news portals, supported and fed by the TV channels and newspapers that have launched them. Alongside these, the practice of 'weblogs' or blogging has also been growing, and slowly, digital cameras, e-mail, camera phones and broadband connectivity opened up hitherto undreamt of vistas and news pools for Hindi.

The twenty-first century Hindi news media is caught in a paradox. India has more varieties of language journalism visible across a wider range of media than at any other time in the past. And Hindi print is still registering a steady growth in numbers, as also its ad revenues. But for journalists, things are not so clear-cut yet. A mightier storm is brewing in the internet-driven media, where digital technology is creating newer global platforms each year, each more capable than the previous one of delivering both news and advertisements online. In Chapter 5 of this book, several of the early entrants to the Hindi digital media world speak of their early interface with the internet and where they feel things are headed now.

One thing is clear: newsrooms of the future will have leaner, meaner desks, and fewer but well-trained multitaskers in the field. Most large Hindi papers still rely heavily on gutsy but mostly untrained and largely inexperienced freelancers. They may risk their lives to get their exclusive stories across to the readers, but remain vulnerable to vendettas and violence unleashed by parties they expose as corrupt. A lot of them work for several papers and must spend most of their time foraging for ads in local markets for regional editions. In a nation with a large number unemployed or under-employed, finding bright and eager young people to do risky running around without raising ethical questions is not too difficult. But it often results in the local politicians and markets getting promotional stories planted as news. Promising young stringers who have migrated, and live in Delhi, Mumbai or Kolkata, must do so with their own resources and buy their own cars/motorbikes and petrol. Among other things, this book also attempts to provide readers a glimpse of this mostly invisible but hugely important world.

In the new global information ecology, according to a report (KPMG and FICCI 2017), TV ad spending by companies today is 39.3 per cent of their total outlay. Of this, the share of print is a little over 33 per cent. The real growth is now where Hindi products are. The newspapers have not yet faced a serious challenge, only because ad flow models for digital news content channels are still not fully developed in India. And the old, 'legacy' news industry is now realising that many of its former readers have begun taking advantage of free news available on the internet, 24/7. Many readers have themselves chosen to turn content creators. But formal or informal, all contributors of news to Hindi media rely a great deal on search engines, blogs, and lately, Facebook (founded in 2004) and Twitter (founded in 2006) feeds. India's print industry, like the West, is waking up to the painful realisation that paying for news is a fast-evaporating habit. And just as fifth-estate giants like Wikipedia and Google have destroyed the venerable *Encyclopaedia Britannica*, digitised news platforms may slowly squeeze the life out of old-style print, unless it adapts.

Patronage too is changing. No wielders of political power hesitate to use their vast advertising coffers and their official machinery to feed, starve, and ultimately keep the editorials and managers mostly compliant with their political ideologies and governmental policies. Over the first two decades of the twenty-first century, contrarians among Hindi editors have greatly diminished in numbers. Most of those who have remained have accepted a swift corporatisation of the economy and their own company boards, to whom the bottom lines matter more than the headlines. In itself, it is an organic development. But to remain viable and retain the trust of the public, Hindi news media now needs to consciously become more inclined towards verified factual information, not sensational assertions and motivated promotion of products and leaders.

On the positive side, in this new digitised world, the owners are trying to save, and invest in high-tech machinery, e-papers and portals, and news-based programming streamed live in Hindi, and use them effectively. They are, therefore, for the first time looking for skilled multitasking young journalists. They now command, and are being provided with, decent wages and work conditions. The next big question is: How can the Hindi media establishment make their newsrooms enrich their news by becoming more democratic, inclusive and hospitable for women and other marginalised groups? A long over-reliance on a largely upper-caste, male workforce, and stringers picked on the basis of unverified information have resulted in teams that are short on facts, biased against skilled hands from marginalised groups and lacking in proper legal knowledge. They can cause serious damage to professional news structures in the age of 24/7 news by inadvertently filing stories that do not stand up to legal scrutiny and can lead to grave situations.

The other point of concern is underscored by a 2018 report by an international body, Reporters without Borders (2018). It called 2018 the deadliest year on record for journalists, with 384 journalists imprisoned and 60 held hostage. The United Nations Educational, Scientific and Cultural Organisation (UNESCO) also confirms that in that year, at least 99 journalists were killed (UNESCO 2020). The main reason for attacks on Indian journalists (most of them working in vernaculars and reporting from small towns and villages) and their swift incarceration, often without following the necessary legal procedures, is the lack of institutional backup and timely intervention. The 2019 elections have highlighted various fault lines within India's public spaces. Chapters 7 and 8 in the book focus on the times ahead and the need to secure our bases before more jolts come.

The existential questions that the Hindi media faces now are actually common to the media in all Indian languages. Should we all go with the tide and continue to milk advertising revenues? Do we not know that the public space it has created in the past century was swiftly colonised by political and corporate interests with deep pockets and divisive agendas?

Can editorials continue, with any degree of honesty, to care for individual rights and local cultures in view of their own and their owners' proximity to political and corporate lobbyists? By now, we cannot pretend we do not know that their interest in Hindi has less to do with their love for India's vernaculars and a lot more to do with accessing India's regional, vernacular-speaking markets. So can we, in the spirit of mutual give and take, insist they provide us with better and cheaper technology and other facilities for aggregating news on par with their English customers?

Another major worry is: Just how far will our Constitution-given freedom of information and speech stretch if the amendments in media laws, proposed in 2018, were to pass? 'Freedom of opinion,' as the philosopher Hannah Arendt (1954) wrote, 'is a farce unless factual information is guaranteed.' But if the need arises, will civil advocates of freedom of speech and information fight the media's fight beyond a point once again, as they did during the Emergency years?

True improvement requires all media stakeholders to hold a mirror to themselves. During the course of writing this book and going through my notes, talking to colleagues present and past, I have gained many new insights. The trust our countless readers, listeners and viewers have reposed in us, as multilingual journalists writing in Hindi, has strengthened both my own self-esteem and my belief in the powerful inclusivity of India's soul. Hindi journalism has lent me a rare capacity to examine stories from rural areas with humility and understanding, and gauge their worth to the democratic matrix. Acquiring language skills has also helped keep many of us firmly insulated from political indoctrination of a kind that insists on a Sanskritic, upper-caste purity for Hindi media and literature. As the playwright, Václav Havel, addressing the people of Czechoslovakia as their president (on New Year's Day, 1990), said, '[O]nly a person or a nation that is self-confident, in the best sense of the word, is capable of listening to others, accepting them as equals.... Let us try to introduce this kind of self-confidence into the life of our community and, as nations, into our behaviour.'

I owe a special debt of gratitude to my colleagues Pramod Joshi, Harjindar Singh, Prakash Hindustani, Nachiketa Desai, Nidheesh Tyagi and Navneet Gurjar, for generously and willingly sharing material on the growth of Hindi's multi-media industry, the digitisation of our newspapers, and the inside structures and functioning of Hindi's rich multi-media world today. For making it possible for the book to come out despite everything, I'd like to append a special thank you note to my editors, Meghna CN and Proteeti Banerjee, and to the duo of Roopa Sharma at Orient BlackSwan and

Nalini Rajan (Dean of Studies at Asian College of Journalism, and also General Editor, Studies in Journalism), who did a very good job of hand-holding all through three very stressful years, experienced both individually and collectively by all of us.

And I hope for all of you who read this book, that you discover yourself while following the long and winding journey of Hindi and Hindi journalism. That you too will rediscover your mother tongues, forge your own unique style and engage your audiences, just as my generation did. You, the young, are so much better technologically equipped and networked with the rest of the world than we were when we took a leap into the dark waters. We had no tradition, little access to good machines and few mentors within the publishing houses and in the political arena. As we jumped headlong into the deep waters one after another, we were first frightened, then surprised, and finally came up, shaking our heads, dripping with the sheer pleasure that comes with having discovered your own voice, your own stories to tell and a readership out there that is eager to hear them.

1

The Story of Hindi

In India—variously described as a cradle of civilisation and of many ancient religions and languages—print media history cannot be described only in terms of ownership, editorial teams or sales and marketing practices. The writer-translator A. K. Ramanujan (1993) correctly underscores the fact that all Indians grow up multilingual; that the princely clans and the nobles that ruled northern India by turns until the British took over were polyglots. In the north, they were familiar not only with the classical languages, Persian, Arabic and Sanskrit, but they could also converse freely with contemporary writers, artists and artisans, and their multilingual harems in their language, fed by various northern *bolis* (dialects): the Khadi Boli, Braj, Awadhi, Bhojpuri, Maithili, Punjabi and Rajasthani. The 1961 Census reports the existence of 1,652 languages in India (RGCCI 1961). According to the 2001 Census, at least 29 of these are spoken by over a million people (RGCCI 2001), of which Hindi has the largest coverage, including 11 northern states. Today, after Mandarin, Hindi is spoken by the largest group, of some 570 million Indians.

THE MAKING OF HINDI INTO A FORMAL LANGUAGE

Pre-colonial India had multiple knowledge traditions. Till about 200 years ago, what we call 'Hindi' today was known as 'Hindavi', an oral vernacular tradition used by all ordinary Indians in the northern plains, with regional variations. Around the beginning of the nineteenth century, when British officials of the East India Company began looking for a single native language fit for formal communication with the Indian masses of the north, they were guided to Hindi or Hindavi. The terms Hindi and Hindavi were not indigenous, but actually coined by Arabic-speaking peoples from Central Asia. Hordes of them crossed the river Sindhu over the centuries and, there being no sibilant in Arabic, termed the river 'Hindhu', those that lived in the plains across the Hindhu as 'Hindi', and their language as 'Hindavi'. So when the poet-scholar Amir Khusro (1253–1325) compiled the words from the native languages in his dictionary, *Khalik Bari* (1320), he recorded the various hybridised versions of a language called Hindavi, that was used from Punjab to Bihar.

In the seventeenth century, the Portuguese coined another synonym for Hindavi, 'Indostani'. This was later corrupted to 'Hindustani'. The indigenous poets of Hindavi also referred to it as '*Bhakha*' (the spoken word). The term that was used to refer to the four clerks the British set to work on standardising this chameleon language was 'Bhakha *munshis*'. There is no doubt, however, that Hindi, as it was spoken then, sounded no different from Urdu, a hybrid born out of the intermingling of Perso-Arabic-speaking army camps and ordinary natives in and around the Red Fort area in Delhi. The construct of Hindi-Hindu and Urdu-Muslim literary traditions and political definitions was created much later and had nothing to do with literature. Muslim rulers and their court scribes, up until the early nineteenth century, recorded most Hindi and Urdu works in the Perso-Arabic script. Only a few Hindi writers used the Indic Dev Nagari script used by Sanskrit scholars. Some Hindu scribes also used Kaithi, a script limited to account-keepers and the mercantile class. Many musical compositions for the classical Hindustani music were composed by both Hindu and Muslim musicians who proliferated in the decadent years of the Moghul dynasty and were recorded in the Perso-Arabic-Urdu script. Since these verses were eventually sung or recited aloud in the *durbars* (courts) of the princes, the temples or the village *chaupals* (rural squares where people gather), the recitals posed no problems of comprehension.

This multiplicity of dialects and varieties of Hindavi as it was spoken made standardising the vocabulary and orthography of a formal Hindi a problematic exercise for the British. At the Fort William College (founded in 1800 in Calcutta), the Bhakha munshis picked up the Khadi Boli version of Hindavi as the base for crafting a formal pan-north Indian Hindi language. This is what the Hindi writers and the media used in the following decades. One may ask why, out of so many variants of spoken Hindi, the clerks chose the Khadi Boli as their base. Was it because the Delhi-Agra region had been the erstwhile seat of historical and cultural authority? Or did it have something to do with the fact that the four Bhakha munshis, tasked with producing a formal Hindi for communication with East India Company officials, all hailed from that region? We will never know for sure. What we do know is that by 1920, educated Indians had begun pushing clear literary, political and social agendas through the Fort William College version of Hindi. And soon after that, community identities of Hindus and Muslims began crystallising around Hindi (in the Dev Nagari script) and Urdu (in the Perso-Arabic Rekhta script) as crafted at the Fort William College.

In the north, the large community of Hindus and their increasing identification with Hindi as a vehicle of nationalism received a big boost when major political leaders and social reformers began to use Hindi as the unifier of various national agendas for defining and communicating India's own agenda for progress. Among them were Gujarati-speaking barrister turned public leader, Mohandas K. Gandhi, a prominent Bengali-speaking nobleman-cum-social reformist, Raja Ram Mohun Roy, and a Punjabi, Dayanand Saraswati, founder of the Arya Samaj (1875).

THE BEGINNINGS OF HINDI PRINT TECHNOLOGY IN INDIA

The earliest known specimens of the movable Dev Nagari script were cast in Rome in 1740 (Stark 2008: 35). Movable type, however, entered India only in the late decades of the eighteenth century. Printing had already been introduced in the southern part of India in the sixteenth century by the Jesuit missionaries who had followed Portuguese traders to India's southwestern coast. They had set up the first printing press in Goa, and in the next four years, a printing machine shipped from Portugal was used to print five religious texts in Portuguese. These were meant to serve the needs of the local community of Christians of Portuguese origin camping in the area.

By the late seventeenth century, British East India Company officials, who had established a firm base in India, also felt the need to communicate in local languages for facilitating their trade and revenue collection activities. Under their active encouragement, a press was set up in Calcutta to publish books and Christian tracts in English and Indian languages, first in Bangla and finally, in Hindi and Urdu, the languages widely spoken in the rest of northern India from the Punjab to Bihar, forming almost 40 per cent of the total native population. The movable Dev Nagari type was first used in Calcutta. This city was, by the early nineteenth century, an important trading centre that, under Governor General Warren Hastings, was fast becoming a major centre of Oriental learning as well, with institutions like the Royal Asiatic Society (established 1784) and the Fort William College (established 1800). Encouraged by the Orientalists, in 1789, one of the first commercial presses in Calcutta, the Chronicle Press, printed a miscellany of Asiatic verse (*New Asiatick Miscellany*) which had a few Sanskrit verses and some Rekhta couplets by the Deccan poet, Wali Deccani, in the Nagari script.

Around 1812, as a producer of printed material for mass consumption and a little later as a producer of paper for printing, Calcutta was becoming a hub of real print activity and technical experimentation. The Serampore Press had begun by printing prayer books and tracts in English and Bangla for recent native converts to the Christian faith. But the non-religious papers printed in the north between 1780 and 1818 were all in English. They were not meant for the natives but functioned as a space for disgruntled officials of the Company to air their grievances, meant for the ears of the movers and shakers in Calcutta and London.

Stirrings of Change among the Indian Elite Who Had First Shunned Print

Against this hectic activity, it is strange to think that the northern readers and patrons of literature took several decades to accept books, newspapers and periodicals in the printed form. In the north, texts were prized and were rare collector's items that only the very rich or those coming from a long line of upper-caste, learned men could access. Knowledge of the highest order was treated as a holy secret, only to be imparted orally to carefully chosen acolytes. Texts, when they were written, were written by hand, first on palmyra leaves, then bhoj tree bark, and later, paper. Handwritten manuscripts were carefully guarded items among the upper castes and classes, and royal libraries. The Moghul emperors traditionally had limited copies of beautifully and lavishly illustrated handwritten manuscripts created by royal painters and calligraphers.

By the early nineteenth century, both native Muslim and Hindu rulers began to sense the potential of print technology for creating large groupings of vernacular readers for themselves when they saw how the missionaries were using the native languages to communicate directly with their erstwhile subjects. This exchange of information between the foreigners and their people was happening while their own political and economic power was slipping out of reach and being consolidated in the hands of East India Company officials. The native princes were alarmed at the prospect of losing their Islamic and Hindu identities under the aggressive challenge posed by Christian missionaries, helped and promoted by the Company. They were, however, wary of being openly defiant. An open rebellion could well have resulted in exile and the loss of their pensions and privileges. It was easier to recapture and retain public attention by using the print medium and native languages to keep their native flocks together. This led to several princely houses self-consciously choosing Khadi Boli Hindi as a vehicle of communication and patronising the mass production of texts, pamphlets, periodicals and newspapers in Hindi. The inclusion or exclusion of words from Urdu, Persian and dialects that were part of colloquial Hindi in their areas depended on their culture-specific view of Hindi.

The Fort William College of Calcutta, Where a Formal Hindi was Born

Seeing how the native ruling classes were indifferent to the new movable type and print technology, the British, who were keen to create a uniform, standardised people's language for carrying out major trade and administrative activities, reached out to John Gilchrist (1759–1841). Gilchrist was a Scotsman who had entered the services of the East India Company as an assistant surgeon.

Once the good doctor was appointed as the supervisor of the Hindustani department at the Fort William College, he consulted the ruling native elite about the language question. The Muslim rulers and noblemen told him a courtly, Persianised Urdu formed the top register in the native linguistic scale, and Hindi written in the Nagari script (borrowed from Sanskrit) was but the rustic bottom register of the linguistic repertoire of commoners in the north.

Gilchrist and his posse of four clerks (Bhakha munshis)—Munshi Sadasukhlal, a Kayastha (one of the better educated and multilingual castes among the non-Brahminical Hindus), two Brahmins, Pandit Lallulal and Pandit Sadal Mishra, and one Muslim, Syed Insha Allah Khan—were not particularly bothered about the Indian hierarchies and were focused on the communicability factor. The four Bhakha munshis were finally mandated to standardise both Hindi (in the Nagari script) as the formal language of the Hindus, and Urdu (in the Nastalique, a hybrid of the Perso-Urdu script) as the formal language of the Muslims, for all practical purposes.

To speed up the process of printing tracts and vital papers in Hindi and Urdu, in 1802, Gilchrist also set up the Hindustani Press. It began by printing works in Urdu. As an administrator, Gilchrist recognised the hidden political potential of Hindi in Nagari as a good tool to help craft a separate identity for the numerically larger Hindu populace, that would, in time, set them apart from the numerically smaller Muslim population. To Muslims, Urdu, with its Perso-Arabic script, would become a badge of religious identity combined with notions of courtly elegance. Fort William College, under Gilchrist, was becoming a busy hub that crafted two separate, ethnically-stamped worlds for Hindi and Urdu, which was to have far-reaching consequences.

By the beginning of the twentieth century, Hindi written in the Nagari script came to signify the cultural and religious thinking and aspirations of the Hindus for a whole generation of educated Indians through school texts circulated in the new school system. Urdu, in the Perso-Arabic Rekhta script, similarly became a symbol and a vehicle of the cultural and national aspirations of Muslims. And the two languages, once considered inseparable, became increasingly distanced from each other as markers of two separate races in the north: the Hindus and the Muslims—a fact that was heavily exploited by politically ambitious parties. The trend continued after Gilchrist's untimely death under his successor, William Hunter. The initial impact of the printed works produced by the presses in Calcutta may have been limited outside the college to a tiny circle of Orientalists, but two genres, religious stories (like Lallulal's Hindi *Premsagar*, 1810) and tales or *quissas* (like Mir Amman's Urdu *Bagh o bahar*, 1804), were to become very popular in the following decades as literacy levels rose under the new vernacular school system.

THE IMPACT OF GOVERNMENT SCHOOL TEXTS IN HINDI

By 1860, government schools in the north were teaching a steadily increasing number of young students in the vernacular medium, as per the advice of the historic Wood's Despatch (1854; see Orsini 2002). The annual report of the administration of Oudh for the decade of 1866–76 (see Stark 2008) shows the number of students learning Hindi in the North-Western Provinces and Oudh government schools rising nearly five times, from 7,702 to 34,232. By 1868, Hindi-language publications outnumbered Urdu in the province, though Oudh registered a dominance of Urdu until the third decade of the next century, when Hindi overtook Urdu as the most popular language for print publications. Since business was growing for the vernaculars, a missionary, William Carey, and his Indian helper, Panchanan Karmkar, went on to establish a type foundry for casting typefaces in various Indian languages for the use of Company officials. A similar unit came up in Bombay, where Javaji Dadaji, a Parsi entrepreneur, set up the fabled Nirnay Sagar Press, along with a foundry, Nirnay Sagar Type Foundry. The 'Bombay type' that this press introduced was a more elegant and refined version of the Serampur types.

By 1868, the official registration of printing companies began and by the late 1880s, there were over 110 printing presses, most located in one of the six urban centres in what is now Uttar Pradesh: Allahabad, Lucknow, Benares, Aligarh, Agra and Kanpur. Urdu was the dominant language in the western regions, but the standardisation of Hindi and Urdu introduced an insidious communalisation of scripts that grew and deepened over the next century in the plains of the north. The growth and governmental promotion of Hindi in schools also fed latent regional hostilities between the Bengali-speaking publishers of Calcutta and the migrants who had arrived from the Hindi regions to Calcutta.

PRIVATE INDIAN OWNERSHIP OF PRINT AND THE NAVAL KISHORE PRESS OF OUDH

Over half-a-century (beginning with the North-Western Provinces in 1805 and Uttarakhand after 1857), the British amalgamated the vast Hindi heartland piecemeal. In contrast to the nascent but small, English-educated, bilingual middle class of Bengal, they found that west of Bengal, the Hindus and the Muslims had their own local traditions of teaching and learning, their own caste-class groupings, and attitudes towards religion.

For quite a while, the government remained the biggest investor in vernacular publishing, and backed several privately funded publications launched around this time, but soon faced a big funding crunch. Literacy rates were low and the size of the Hindi-Urdu reading public remained small all through the nineteenth and early twentieth centuries. Private publications depended heavily on the largesse of the princely houses and rich, rural *zemindars* (landlords) in the north, who wanted to flaunt their Hindi-Urdu publications as proof of their being cultured and devout Hindus or Muslims. But gradually, as the textbooks brought forth a new generation of Hindi readers, demand for literary texts and translations of Sanskrit classics began to grow. As the German philosopher Jürgen Habermas (1989) theorised later in his theory of communicative rationality and the public sphere, once print has created a 'bourgeois public sphere', commercial entrepreneurs will follow and begin using the space for commercial purposes. Thus, an early entrant to the Hindi-Urdu space, Munshi Naval Kishore's press, established a year after the 1857 mutiny in Lucknow (the capital of Oudh), soon rose to be one of the most commercially successful early publishers of Hindi-Urdu texts under the British government. Naval Kishore (1836–95), the native owner of a vernacular printing press, became a leading light of not only the publishing industry in north India, but also an effective bridge between the political establishment and the native citizens.

He voiced his conviction (in *The Pioneer*, November 1880) in the theory that after the departure of the East India Company, the vast community of (both literate and illiterate) natives must consider the rule of the British Crown as the sole guarantee of new ideas, progress, peace, and stability in India.

The munshi had good reason to befriend British establishment officials. Activities in the Hindi language, formally standardised by the British Bhakha munshis of the Fort William College, were amply funded by the Company and later by the Crown. The British were, moreover, keen to start a chain of vernacular-medium schools and establish direct communication with the natives to preclude any possibility of another popular uprising against the rulers. This guaranteed that the popular vernaculars, Urdu and Hindi, became the sole languages of official communication and of school texts that the Naval Kishore Press was ready to print. In the venture, Raja Shiv Prasad 'Sitara e Hind', a Varanasi nobleman who had been appointed as the inspector of schools by the Crown in the Oudh area and was known to be an early promoter of Hindi, also proved to be a good native ally.

Some Initial Problems of Printing in Vernaculars

In the early years of the nineteenth century, the German technique of lithography (a technique that employed reproducing the printed word by transferring it to a stone surface before printing) was introduced in Calcutta. It gave a big boost to printing texts in India, especially Urdu, whose discursive calligraphy could be perfectly reproduced by this technique. By 1826, a lithography press had also came up in Patna, and in the next three decades, more works were lithographed in India than in Europe (Stark 2008: 45). Lithography was followed by the replacement of the wooden press with the iron printing press. This was quickly adopted in India. This was carried a step further by the invention of the steam-powered cylindrical press in Germany in the early nineteenth century. It raised the output substantially, but was adopted more slowly in India as it was more expensive than the manually operated press.

The indigenous paper industry too began registering growth at this point in India, beginning with the government-owned Serampur Paper Mill. By 1880, Naval Kishore, the prolific printer of Lucknow, had also established the Lucknow Paper Mills and became the chief supplier of indigenous newsprint to printers in Oudh, Punjab, right up to the northwestern areas. The Hindi-speaking area in the nineteenth century was a vast region that stretched from what is now Rajasthan to Bihar in the east, from the Punjab and Uttarakhand in the north, and the Central Provinces up to Berar. And as the popular saying went, this was an area where the water and the spoken language changed after each 5 *kos* (some 10 kilometres). When multiple-language print activity began, the targeted native areas were revealed to have many caste-based variations in their levels of literacy, which also stretched to their socio-cultural attitudes and led to wide variations in the market consumption of print.

UDANT MARTAND, HINDI'S FIRST PAPER WITH A VERY SHORT LIFE

According to a statement (titled 'Native Public', included in the parliamentary papers, 1931, for the British governments of Bengal and Bombay Presidencies; see Stark 2008) of 9 February 1826, one Jugal Kishore Shukla applied to C. Lushington, chief secretary to the government, stating that he was 'desirous of publishing a weekly newspaper in the Hindee language and Deo Nagree characters to be entitled, *Oodunt Martand*', and forwarded the requisite affidavit, verified by himself and Munnoo Thakur, to a magistrate for the government's authority and sanction under the 1823 Press Ordinance. The licence was duly issued on 16 February 1826. It was thus that 10 May 1826 became a historic day in the life of print publications in Hindi. This was the day the first newspaper in Hindi and Urdu, the *Udant Martand* (The Rising Sun), saw the light of day. As per information given in its print line, the paper was launched in Calcutta from a printing press located in house number 37, in Amadatalla Lane, Kolhu Tola, Calcutta. The founding editor was Shukla, originally a native of Kanpur in Uttar Pradesh. Like many fortune-seekers in the north, Shukla had chosen to settle in Calcutta, where he began as a clerk in the Calcutta court and later became a lawyer. An editorial written by him for the first issue (30 May 1826) sets out the paper's aim of serving the vernacular reading public by providing them with truthful reporting and enlightening them about public welfare projects patronised by the Governor General. This eight-page paper was priced at Rs 2. *Udant Martand* unfortunately had a short life, a year and seven months, and was closed down in December 1827 after having published a total of 79 issues. The main reason for its closure was paucity of funds. The immediate reason, however, was a case of defamation lodged in the Supreme Court against Shukla by another publisher, Bhawani Charan Banerji. Faced with a court notice, Shukla found neither the requisite support nor funds from his readers, a small community of Hindi-speaking traders. The venture thus ended rather messily for him. He was declared a bankrupt entrepreneur and his properties were seized by the court.

HINDI SCHOOL TEXTS AND THE RISE OF VARANASI AND LUCKNOW AS PUBLISHING HUBS

Raja Shiv Prasad 'Sitara e Hind', a decorated nobleman and eminent citizen of Varanasi, was the inspector of schools to the government in the United Provinces (now Uttar Pradesh). He rose to be a prolific writer of Hindi textbooks. In January 1845, he also helped Yadunath Thatte, a Maharashtrian Brahmin, to bring out *Banaras Akhbar*, which the then king of Nepal supported financially. This monthly newspaper, priced at Rs 1 per copy, was published from Varanasi using the newly introduced German lithographic technique. Varanasi, a city known as a seat of traditional learning, always had a population with noticeably high literacy rates and a mixed population comprising of scholars from various parts of India. Varanasi also traditionally marked the beginning of Hindi publishing in the Hindi heartland. Its *Banaras Akhbar* discarded the Calcuttan (Kalkatiya) Hindi of the short-lived Calcutta Hindi paper, *Udant Martand*, and promoted the colloquial Hindi laced with Urdu that was spoken and understood in the Hindi area from Varanasi to Lahore. *Banaras Akhbar* featured local news, and also serialised some Sanskrit law texts, translated into easy-to-understand Hindi. These texts were greatly in demand among those who aspired to join an increasingly lucrative profession in law, but were not well-versed in Sanskrit. Encouraged by the success of his Hindi paper, Thatte also brought out an Urdu monthly, *Banaras Gazette*. But earnings from both vernaculars remained slim, and by 1854, both these papers had folded up.

As the case of Thatte's papers makes clear, in the nineteenth century, there was a fair amount of enthusiasm about printed Hindi and Urdu texts, but little market support, as most Hindi-Urdu readers were not well-off. A rival press in Varanasi, Sudhakar Press (established 1847), too, faced similar hiccups. It was heavily subsidised by the maharaja of Benares, and later by the government, which by now was fully aware of the potential of the vernacular press. The reason for its failure was that it used a chaste, Sanskritised Hindi that did not find favour with the common readers. The paper tried printing bilingual columns in Hindi and Urdu but the size of the readership and their purchasing power remained poor, and by the mid-1850s, the press was printing only books.

ROYAL PATRONAGE FOR HINDI IN THE NINETEENTH CENTURY AS A BADGE OF NATIONAL IDENTITY

In 1893, three young students in Varanasi, Shyam Sundar Das, Ramnath Mishra and Thakur Shiv Kumar Singh, founded the Nagari Pracharini Sabha, with the stated twin objectives of promoting Hindi literature and also the Dev Nagari script. They were soon noticed by the princely houses who were, at the time, the chief patrons of print periodicals. A few years later, in 1900, a delegation of Indian princes, including Balwant Singh, the raja of Awagarh, Ram Prasad Singh, the raja of Manda, Pratap Narayan Singh, the raja of Ayodhya, and the Congress stalwart, Madan Mohan Malaviya, a lawyer and editor, called upon the Viceroy to request that Hindi be used as the native language in the courts in north India. This led to a resolution in 1900 that ordained that Hindi be used alongside Urdu in the courts in the north, as these were the only languages the public understood.

As the idea of a community of Hindi speakers caught the imagination of the native princes and princelings, several Hindi papers using the Nagari script were launched under their indulgent, though rather laid-back, patronage. To them, the use of Hindi was more of a symbolic self-assertion of their Hindu identity. It also assuaged a certain guilt many of them carried for having surrendered before an alien power. The papers they helped launch were marked by an acute awareness of the value of literacy and a desire to gain access to the revered printed word, which had so far been a protected area within the reach of only the upper castes and classes. In their increasing zeal to create a public sphere for the vernaculars, industrialists, royal patrons of the arts and literature, educators and social reformers slowly drew together and began to operate within the new Hindi public sphere.

The landed gentry also joined this august club. In 1829, the *Bengal Herald* proprietors, for example, included celebrities such as the brothers Dwarakanath and Prasanno Coomar Thakur from the wealthy Tagore family, and eminent social reformer, Raja Ram Mohun Roy. Apart from their Bengali publications, they also chose to bring out a Hindi weekly, *Bangdoot* (The Messenger from Bengal), to communicate with the Hindi public. It published articles by Roy on his religious beliefs and his opinions on several social reforms that Hindu society needed urgently. Outside Bengal, Raja Laxman Prasad of Agra also brought out *Praja Hitaishi* (founded in 1861), a bilingual paper (in Hindi and Urdu), and Raja Rampal Singh of Kalakankar launched *Hindusthan* in 1883 (edited by Madan Mohan Malaviya). The maharaja of Rewa in Bundelkhand, Baldeo Singh ju Dev, also helped publish *Bharat Bhrata*.

Bharatendu Harishchandra, a Brilliant Maverick

An eminent scion of an Agarwal family of traders in Varanasi, Bharatendu Harishchandra suddenly zoomed in on this scene. He was himself a writer of repute, vastly interested in getting the printed word in Hindi and the writings of Vaishnava saint-poets closer to the community. To this end, he supported Hindustani, a secular Hindi that was different from Urdu only by the Nagari script it used. It was colloquial, witty, and laced with several northern dialects—Urdu, Persian, and even a few English words. Bharatendu was a delightful figure: a rich, eccentric dandy, a patron of courtesans, and a talented young writer and editor with easy access to both money and publishers. On 15 August 1867, he launched a self-edited periodical, *Kavi Vachan Sudha*. His editorial declared that this was a refined version of a hybrid Hindi that alone could carry new ideas to readers: *Hindi naye chaal mein dhalee* (Hindi recast in a modern form). A rake, a renowned patron of art and music, and a great good-time Charlie, this creative talent died young of consumption at the age of 32. But during his meteoric career, he demolished many linguistic and socio-cultural shibboleths and left behind a memorable collection of magazines (*Harishchandra*, launched 1873, and *Balabodhini*, a women's monthly, launched 1874), several collections of essays, plays, satires and a body of poems on devotion and carnal love.

In Bharatendu, nineteenth-century Hindi found a loud, intelligent iconoclast who pushed aside the formal, ethnic straitjacketing that the Fort William College Orientalists had devised for Hindi as a language of Hindus. He created a canon for Hindi that used the Nagari script, but remained liberal, inclusive and accommodative. He underscored Khusro's (1320) observation in the fourteenth century that India spoke Hindavi, a mélange of languages and dialects, impossible to replicate in official Persian or Sanskrit. Bharatendu wrote in his editorials that no less than 12 kinds of Hindi were commonly used in the northern plains from the Punjab to Bengal, including a variety he called 'Railway Hindi'—Hindi flecked with English and Anglo-Indian terms. The great flowering of Hindi as a hybrid that followed in the early decades of the twentieth century and its nationalist secular press would have been unthinkable without a pathbreaker like him.

METAL MOULDS AND NATIVE TECHNOLOGICAL INNOVATIONS

Around the 1880s, metal moulds were invented for printing in Europe. This was a technique basically developed for a limited number of roman fonts. When this was introduced in India, where the printing industry was still learning to walk, Indian printers faced several challenges vis-à-vis the vernaculars. Both Urdu and Hindi were non-roman scripts and required the manufacturing of many more types and typographical designs for the phonetic Indic scripts. Urdu Hindi letters have ornate shapes and need many more typefaces as symbols for each letter in its variations for expressing a unique spoken sound (*maatra*). These problems complicated not only the processes of composition, but also readying the completed forms (popularly referred to as 'ferma') for reproduction. All this required both time and money. And since they were not easy to procure initially, the fonts available for printing Hindi newspapers and periodicals remained unattractive right up to the 1970s, even though the English papers with bigger budgets were sprucing up their printing regularly using imported Linotype and Monotype machinery.

By the late nineteenth century, the readership for print periodicals and tracts, and localised information had grown beyond Varanasi to other Hindi-speaking states. During this phase, we had several short-lived periodicals and papers, like the Hindi Urdu *Malwa Akhbar* of Indore (published in Indore at Maharaja Holkar's printing press), the Bengali Hindi *Sudha Varshan* (a daily published by a Bengali, Shyam Sundar Sen, of Calcutta), another Hindi Urdu publication, *Rajputana Akhbar* (Jaipur, 1856), the weekly *Jagat Hitkaaraka* (Lucknow, 1861), *Almora Akhbar* (Almora, in what is now Uttarakhand, 1871), which was published by a local debating club and was closed down in 1918 by the British, whose *kuli begar* (recruitment for free porters) practices it opposed, and *Bharat Mitra* (a weekly launched in 1878 that became a daily, and lasted till 1907), backed by a social reformer and proponent of Dayanand Saraswati and Bharatendu Harishchandra. Ironically, *Bharat Mitra* was taken over by the right-wing Varnashram Sangh of Kashi, who sacked its charismatic Gandhian editor, Laxmi Narayan Garde, who started the trend of interviewing celebrities with an interview with Gandhi during his visit to Kashi. It closed down in 1934.

The Vernacular Press Act and the Beginning of Government Censorship

By the late nineteenth century, the British government was sufficiently alarmed by the rising tones of aggressive 'nationalist' sentiments in language papers to bring in the notorious Vernacular Press Act of 1878. This Act gave the government the power to confiscate the assets of vernacular papers, including their presses. A few decades later, it was used liberally to close down papers suspected of seditious writings against the British government. In 1881, Hindi replaced Urdu in the courts in Bihar. This measure led to disaffection in the legal circles that used Urdu and triggered a chain of communalised thinking that saw Hindi as the language of the majority Hindus, favoured unduly by the colonial government, and Urdu as the language of the Muslims. The first four decades of the twentieth century, especially the period between 1920 and 1940, saw a gradual expansion and strengthening of the processes set into motion in the 1890s, including a certain disaffection between Hindus and Muslims, who saw Urdu and Hindi as two separate markers of culture and community. The year 1920 also brought what Francesca Orsini (2002) describes as 'a qualitative leap' that ushered in bold experimentation, new genres and a host of independent writers, many of whom were consciously taking a public role for the first time in those heady and politically exciting times.

Hindi Papers and Periodicals in the Early Twentieth Century

The average Hindi editor at the beginning of the twentieth century was a multilingual man, who spanned the divide between urban and rural audiences, and apart from Hindi, was also familiar with English, Urdu, various local Hindi dialects (bolis) and often, Bengali, given its centrality in the print industry in north India. The mostly British-owned, English-language newspapers, as Jawaharlal Nehru (1936) points out in his autobiography, were full of the doings of high officials and their social lives in big cities and hill stations, and carried long articles on the balls and amateur theatre they delighted in. In contrast, the Hindi papers were addressing popular and politically sensitive audiences, that comprised of factory workers, traders, teachers, clerks, and lower government functionaries like the Patwaris and the Kanungo. They competed fiercely with the already established Urdu to become common currency as publications, and as the medium for formal communication between the government and the common citizens. Some princely families, small zemindars and scions of prosperous farming clans, whose children were sent to Lucknow, Varanasi or Allahabad to study law, also emerged as champions of Hindi. These early pioneers in the Hindi newspaper world, however, used the terms 'rashtra' (nation) and 'jati' (caste, but more specifically, cultural identity) as markers for progress and set about creating a large cultural community with diverse cultural and religious traditions.

HINDI JOURNALS AND THEIR PATRONS

The Hindi press, the Hindi-medium schools, literary genres such as novels and plays, literary associations like the Nagari Pracharini Sabha of Varanasi, now rose as public spaces where ideas on culture and politics were reshaped. Hindi as a hybrid, promoted earlier by Bharatendu and Balmukund Gupt, was further honed and stylised by literary critics like Mahavir Prasad Dwivedi and popularised by editors of publications such as *Aaj* (1920), *Aryavarta* (1940) and *Hindustan* (1936).

Habermas, a German philosopher, had predicted that the newspaper revolution in Europe would be the coming together of private citizens as a 'public', who would then share a common language to create an intermediary space for free public discussions and exchanges of ideas (Habermas 1989). But his views on early publishing were based on the socio-political factors shaping Europe in the eighteenth century. The Indian reality during the same period was quite different. Each group of writers, newspaper owners, editors, readers and contributors who joined the profession viewed events and ideas filtered through their own sense of caste and community, which had shaped and supported socio-political interactions in India's Hindi belt for centuries. One's caste and social status together determined their use of a Sanskritised or hybridised version of Hindi. They also created and sustained various editorial hierarchies within newspaper offices. This many-layered, literate Hindi public of the early twentieth century bears little resemblance to the self-confident bourgeoisie of Habermas, united by a single language, and tolerant and patiently receptive of views other than their own.

When groups of nationalists, protesting against colonial inequality, and social reformers made Hindi language their vehicle

Table 1.1   Some Important Periodicals in the United Provinces, 1920–37

Name of publication	Periodicity	Print run					Price per annum
		1921	1926	1930	1935	1937	(Rs annas)
Abhyuday	Weekly	6,000	3,000	3,000	2,500	6,000	3.8
Aaj	Daily	2,000	3,000	5,000	5,000	6,000	12.0
Bharat	Bi-weekly	-	-	9,000	5,500	5,000	20.0
Bhavisya	Weekly	2,000	-	11,000	-	-	-
Chaand	Monthly	-	6,000	15,000	6,500	5,000	6.8
Hans	Monthly	-	-	1,500	2,000	1,000	6.0
Hindi Kesari	Weekly	3,600	700	3,000	5,000	300	2.4
Madhuri	Monthly	-	6,000	4,000	2,000	2,000	6.8
Pratap	Weekly	9,000	7,500	16,000	14,000	1,000	3.6
Sainik	Weekly	-	1,000	4,500	7,000	5,000	3.0
Saraswati	Monthly	4,000	3,200	3,500	2,500	5,000	3.0
Shakti	Weekly	1,000	1,500	-	1,000	1,200	2.8
Sudha (for women)	Monthly	-	-	7,200	2,000	2,000	12.0
Svades	Weekly	3,500	1,200	-	-	-	-
Vartman	Daily	8,000	2,500	4,000	4,000	2,500	12.0

Source: 'Statement of Newspapers and Periodicals published in the UP', Government Press, Allahabad, for the relevant years. Reprinted in Orsini (2002).

for communication, Hindi became a symbol of political resistance against the British and the Queen's English. But social inequalities remained. English meant better pay, more visibility among the movers and shakers, and two major avenues for employment for the Hindi-educated young, teaching and journalism, remained poorly paid vis-à-vis English practitioners of the same vocations. This further hardened many of the professional users of Hindi towards English and the English-speaking natives, which continues till date in various forms.

Writing for and about the nationalist movement or doubling up as political activists, the Hindi media practitioners of the period between 1920 and 1940 were a mobile young band of committed workers. A few journalists, like Malaviya, Hemvati Nandan Bahuguna and Kamalapati Tripathi, gained positions within the Congress party and rose to be powerful political leaders. But most were content to be part-time political activists. Under their editorial guidance, the Hindi papers began to be seen as the authentic voice of the freedom movement and the public sphere began widening everywhere.

AND THEN COMES MOHANDAS K. GANDHI

Around 1920, the publishing of newspapers to create a public forum received a huge boost with the arrival of Mohandas K. Gandhi from South Africa. Most stalwarts of India's freedom movement, like Gandhi, Malaviya and Bal Gangadhar Tilak, also caught on and launched Hindi papers and periodicals to reach out to the Hindi-speaking masses of northern and central India and carry to them the new concept of 'swaraj' (self-rule) and Indian nationalism. Gandhi had had a long and close association with English-language newspapers in South Africa. In India, he saw merit in bringing out publications in local languages to address the masses who had no access to English. Gandhi's autobiography, *The Story of My Experiments with Truth* (1977 [1927]), tells readers about the circumstances that led to his taking over two newspapers, *Young India* in English and *Navjivan* in Gujarati, then in Hindi. The year was 1919, the place, Ahmedabad, and Gandhi had just arrived in India from South Africa, ready to launch his civil disobedience movement. There were flagrant violations of justice against innocent civilians after the Jallianwalla Bagh massacre in Punjab, and Gandhi wished to visit Punjab immediately but was held back.

To expound the theory of *satyagraha* (policy of standing up for the Truth) to the Indian public in a language they could follow, Gandhi looked around for publications he could take over and edit. Three friends, Umar Sobhani, Shankerlal Banker and Indulal Yagnik of Sabarmati, whom Gandhi's grandson, Rajmohan Gandhi (2006: 226–27), describes as 'three of the Sabarmati covenanters', offered him the editorship of their English journal, *Young India*, and the Gujarati monthly, *Navjivan Ane Satya*, as twin vehicles for communication in vernaculars, which he could turn into weeklies. The original title for the vernacular, *Navjivan Ane Satya*, was changed to just *Navjivan*.

Gandhi writes,

> I was anxious to expound the inner meaning of Satyagraha to the public.... I therefore readily accepted the suggestion made by these friends.
>
> But how could the general public be trained in Satyagraha through the medium of English? My principal field of work lay in Gujarat. Indulal Yagnik ... was conducting the Gujarati monthly *Navajivan* which had the financial backing of these friends. They placed the monthly at my disposal.... This monthly was converted into a weekly.... To have published the two weeklies from two different places would have been very inconvenient to me.... As *Navajivan* was already being published from Ahmedabad, *Young India* was also removed there at my suggestion....
>
> [S]uch journals needed a press of their own.... [T]he existing printing presses ... would have hesitated to publish them.... [T]his could be conveniently done only at Ahmedabad....
>
> [T]hese journals helped also to some extent to remain at peace with myself.... [I] feel that both the journals rendered good service to the people in this hour of trial, and did their humble bit towards lightening the tyranny of the martial law. (Gandhi 1977 [1927])

Within a year of becoming a weekly, the circulation of the Gujarati *Navjivan* had gone up to 20,000, writes the veteran editor, Vijaydutt Shridhar (2008, 2: 625). This further convinced Gandhi that more publications were needed in Indian languages. So two years later, on 19 August 1921, when the Swadeshi Andolan was well entrenched and imported clothes were being burnt in public, Navjivan Mudranalaya (press) also began publishing a Hindi version of *Navjivan*.

Gandhi's *Navjivan* was closed down several times by the British for publishing writings considered seditious. It was a pugnacious paper, and when the government confiscated the book *Hindi Reader*, by Pandit Ramdas Gaur, on charges of sedition, *Navjivan* criticised the action as illegal and unacceptable. On 10 April 1930, Gandhi wrote in *Navjivan* that total swaraj is our birthright. Soon, he was in Yervada jail. On 4 February 1931, the press was seized by the government and both *Young India* and the Hindi *Navjivan* closed down. Once released, they began publishing from Pune under the auspices of the Harijan Sevak Sangh, funded by G. D. Birla (see Shridhar 2019).

Two of Gandhi's widely read books, *Satyagraha in South Africa* (1968 (1928]) and *The Story of My Experiments with Truth* (1977 [1927]), were first serialised in *Navjivan* in Gujarati and then in *Young India* between 1925 and 1929. From 1926–27, the discourses Gandhi gave on the Gita were also serialised in *Navjivan*. When Gandhi was jailed in the mid-1930s, he asked Nehru to ensure that these publications continued. The Gujarati *Navjivan* closed down again in 1948.

Interestingly, in 1930, the Madras-based Gandhian, B. S. Murthy, took Gandhi's vision for Indian languages forward to the south and brought out a Telugu journal, named *Navjivan*. It was priced at 1 anna per copy, and the annual subscription was Rs 4.

CASTE-SPECIFIC HINDI PAPERS

Around the time Gandhi was promoting the vernaculars, over 150 Hindi publications sprang up in Hindi-speaking areas, though most had a short life. Many, like the *Brahmin* of Varanasi (1906), *Jain Hitaishi* of Mumbai, *Kshatriya Samachar* of Patna (1911), *Kayastha Patrika* and *Kayastha Samachar*, catered to specific caste groups and their community interests. The Brahmins and Kayasthas had had higher literacy rates than others and most editors of Hindi publications were Brahmins or Kayasthas. Political leaders like Tilak, however, rose above caste and communal groupings, and were defiantly critical of the policies of the colonial British government for Indians of all castes and regions.

Tilak's fabled daily, *Kesari*, launched a Hindi version from Nagpur and Kashi. By the 1920s, both Hindi dailies were closed down by the British government under the Vernacular Press Act, 1878. Interestingly, some native princely houses also used censorship powers to ban vernacular papers critical of them. In 1920, the princely state of Udaipur banned the Hindi *Rajasthan Kesari* for publishing a scurrilous article about the lavish lives of the maharajas. But all bans and closures led to more dissident and nationalist voices. One such voice was the daily, *Aaj*, published from Varanasi, which declared on its masthead that for the enslaved, there can be no happiness even when asleep (*Paraadheen sapanehu sukh nahin*). The fiery editor of *Aaj*, Baburao Vishnu Paradkar, was arrested and jailed in 1942, but returned in 1947 to edit the paper briefly before his death.

Pratap, another nationalist weekly newspaper, was launched in the newly industrialised city of Kanpur (on 9 November 1913). It was edited by the charismatic Ganesh Shankar Vidyarthi, who led a sustained attack on the divisive policies of the colonial government and the slow communalisation of Hindus and Muslims in the north. *Pratap* was printed from the Pratap Press and had four partners: Ganesh Shankar Vidyarthi, Shiv Narayan Mishra, Yashodanandan of Coronation Press, and Narayan Prasad Arora (Shridhar 2008, Vol. 2: 572). Within two years, the paper was being hounded by the government, and the press and the editors' homes were routinely raided by the police. In 1920, *Pratap* became a daily. It went on to support the peasant movement in Raebareli and refused to apologise when it received a legal notice. In 1921, the editor, Vidyarthi, was sent to prison, and *Pratap* once again became a weekly, edited now by another political activist, Srikrishna Dutt Paliwal, for the next two years. He was followed by the Hindi poet, Makhanlal Chaturvedi. In March 1924, Vidyarthi took charge as editor once again and began to write against the blatant use of religion by the British and their stooges to create disaffection among the ill-informed and under-educated Hindu and Muslim masses in the north. An editorial against a particularly high-handed police inspector published in *Pratap* in 1926 once again led to the paper being served a court notice, and an order by the district court to pay a fine of Rs 400 or serve a six-month jail sentence, later waived by the high court. In 1930, *Pratap* wrote against the Press Ordinance that the British had brought in and the press had to be shut down. On 25 March 1931, when Kanpur was facing violent communal riots after the hanging of three young men, Sukhdev Thapar, Shivaram Rajguru and Bhagat Singh, Vidyarthi visited the city to try and douse the fires of communalism and was killed by anonymous hands. *Pratap* changed several editors thereafter.

With Gandhi's message gaining ground and a rise in Hindi literacy, smaller towns began to publish periodicals. Among them was *Shakti* of Almora, a small hill town in Uttarakhand that Gandhi had visited, and where he had written his famous tract on *anasakti* (total detachment) (Gandhi 2014 [1929]). In 1918, Badridutt Pande, a local lawyer, became the founding editor of *Shakti*. He also went to jail for a year in 1921 and again in 1931.

By the 1930s, the frequently jailed Gandhi wished for all three publications he had launched to be merged into *Harijan* and be published under this generic name. So the Hindi *Navjivan* was dubbed '*Harijan Sevak*' and soon become the mouthpiece of Gandhi and the Indian National Congress party. At this point, Gandhi asked his friend and supporter, the industrialist Birla, to support the venture. He wished particularly to focus on the issue of Harijans in Indian society and the menace of the caste system as it existed and oppressed the Harijan community. Thus, in 1933, three journals, in English (*Harijan*), Gujarati (*Harijan Bandhu*) and Hindi (*Harijan Sevak*), were brought out. All three papers and their editors were regularly penalised and punished for the liberal debate that most Indian-owned language dailies were carrying out.

Gandhi Hands Over His Print Legacy to Nehru

The above three papers were seen as the authentic vehicle for communicating Gandhian thoughts and directives for the Satyagraha movement. It was a period full of turmoil, with the repeated incarceration of all major leaders, including Gandhi, by the colonial government. In the late 1930s, Nehru founded the Associated Journals Ltd., consolidating the Gandhian legacy of public-oriented journalism further into an independent India. The

Congress Committee created a number of units based on Indian languages, including one for Hindustani written in the Nagari script, which Gandhi saw as a mixing bowl for various Indian languages and dialects, and pronounced it a countrywide lingua franca. This was firmly opposed by both Bangla-speaking Subhash Bose and Tamil-speaking C. Rajagopalachari.

While the weekly and daily newspapers were creating a public space for political discourse, a few Hindi magazines were servicing the cause of refining Hindi Khadi Boli, making it both colloquial and acceptable to literary writers who had mostly been writing in the dialects. Some of these were the monthly *Indu* (published in 1909 by the poet Jaishankar Prasad), *Madhuri*, a magazine from the vast stables of the Naval Kishore Press of Lucknow (launched in 1922 and went on to publish till 1950), and *Chaand* (launched in 1922 by Ramrakh Singh Sehgal), a monthly that earned much renown and drew the ire of the government for bringing out 'Faansi ank', an issue that focused on the martyrs hanged by the British (published as a Diwali issue, November 1928). It was soon confiscated as it lauded those who had been hanged on charges of sedition. It closed down in 1939.

The caste and communal groupings, however, still mattered and were honed to a new kind of sharpness by the increasing separation of the Indian public into Hindus and Muslims. In 1925, the Bharatiya Hindu Shuddhi Sabha of Agra brought out *Shuddhi Samachar*, and the following year, the historic Kalyan Press of Poddar was established and began publishing the *Kalyan* magazine, which became hugely popular among Hindus for the translated versions of Sanskrit texts and commentaries on the Sanatan religion. In 1936, a Jain publication, *Jain Dhwaj*, was launched from Ajmer in Rajasthan, and the same year, a group of Marwari students living in Calcutta launched *Marwadi*, a periodical that published in English and Hindi. Contrary to *Pratap* and *Kesari*, these publications set out to promote and underscore clear notions of boundaries around caste, class and regional groupings.

That was the beginning of a clash of political titans over the question of a national ethos and a national language for India. Gandhi favoured the use of Hindustani, a hybrid spoken by the largest number of Indians. But the debates in the Constituent Assembly (1946–49) on this issue were marked by unsettling acrimony and dissent. In 1950, after a long, argumentative session, the makers of India's Constitution endorsed Gandhi's view that Hindi should be the official language of independent India, with English continuing as an associate official language for another 15 years (see Misra 2019). Many members from non-Hindi states felt this threatened their regional identities and immediately disagreed. On 25 January 1965, a day before the mandated 15-year period for English was to end, widespread anti-Hindi riots broke out in Madras state. Students and Dravida Munnetra Kazhagam (DMK) leaders led India's non-Hindi speaking states into opposing what they have since seen as the imperialist design of the Hindi-speaking north to subserviate all other linguistic and ethnic identities. The ruling Congress government hastily amended the orders, allowing English to continue indefinitely till Hindi became acceptable to all states, thereby guaranteeing virtually indefinite bilingualism, but the damage was done. The Congress party never regained political power in Tamil Nadu.

Until India gained freedom, major Indian businesses rarely showed any inclination towards owning a paper, particularly in Indian languages. It was not deemed a profitable venture. The jute baron Birla was an exception, but he, as a close friend of Gandhi's, was prompted into taking charge of the *Harijan* while Gandhi was in and out of jail, and later brought out the *Hindustan Times* in 1926, and two decades later, again at Gandhi's prompting, a Hindi sister daily, *Hindustan*.

INDEPENDENCE AND A DEEPENING OF UNEASE

The first five prime ministers of India were all from the demographically dominant Hindi belt, and in parliamentary debates, several combative supporters of Hindi, such as P. D. Tandon and Dr Raghuvir, put off many by insisting on purging Hindi of all 'foreign' words and developing it as a Sanskritised language for the entire nation (see Misra 2019). Then, there was the Hindu Mahasabha, the parent organisation of what we now call the Sangh Parivar, whose xenophobic support for 'Hindi-Hindu-Hindustan' seemed to many another conspiracy to use language to divide the nation along caste and communal lines. Many little politicians with big political ambitions, keen on building a USP for themselves as saviours of the culture of the masses, also chose to ride the anti-Hindi bandwagon. They were supported by bureaucrats who did not wish to leave their own English comfort zones, some Indo-Anglian writers who had earned some degree of fame in Europe, and academics. They all swiftly blamed Hindi for various ills, from communal tensions to poor quality of public education, to justify their own monolingual careers.

By the time India won freedom, journalistic writing and the language used had become a political act. In 1947, on the occasion of the first meeting of the Hindi Sahitya Sammelan post-Independence, Tandon said to the audience that if they wanted to be nationalists, they must unitedly stand under the banner of one nation, one language, one script and one culture (see Orsini 2002). This rejection of the essential pluralism of India's basic ethos, the extreme reluctance to let dissenters, critics and opponents of uniformity have a space is being reproduced seven decades later by the Bharatiya Janata Party (BJP). Most Indo-Anglian journalists and writers at this point refused to accept that Hindi was actually mirroring deep social and cultural fault lines that ran right under the entire political edifice in north India. Making Hindi a medium of instruction and removing English from government school syllabi was not a public-spirited act but a politically motivated one, and carried assumptions about caste, class and religion and a push for homogenisation. It is because of this recurrently surfacing, narrow definition of both language and nationalism that our non-Hindi states and the national media have come to treat Hindi as a regional and culturally loaded language, incapable of handling national and international political discourse, or even science and technology.

In the following chapters, we will try and see how the Hindi public sphere and its readership has expanded steadily in the second half of the twentieth century, how the deep sense of unease over Hindi, especially down south and in the east, has been handled, and issues that Hindi writers and journalists have supported and clashed over with political parties and their leaders—in brief, the making and unmaking of news and newspapers at the turn of the century.

Conclusion

Hindi, written in the Dev Nagari script as we know it today, was first crafted as a formal language early in the nineteenth century, at the behest of East India Company officials at the Fort William College in Calcutta. Variously known till then as Hindustani, Hindavi or Indostani, this hybridised mass language was identical to Urdu, and its poetic and musical lyrics were mostly written using the Persian script. Under orders from the British, the four clerks tasked with creating two separate vernaculars for the Hindus and the Muslims crafted Hindi and Urdu, by borrowing the Dev Nagari script for Hindi and developing the Nastalique script for Urdu, which was a Perso-Arabic script with a few changes to include the uniquely spoken sounds of Hindavi, the language of the northern plains. The Hindi heartland remained indifferent to the new print technology introduced first by the Portuguese and adopted later by the British, largely for printing and distributing religious texts for native converts to Christianity. Around 1826, Jugal Kishore Shukla, a Hindu from Uttar Pradesh settled in Calcutta, launched India's first Hindi paper in the Nagari script, using the lithographic technique. This paper, as also another one published in Varanasi, the heart of traditional learning, that marked the beginning of the Hindi era, closed soon due to lack of financial support.

Things perked up for Hindi in the post-mutiny years after the Crown took over from the Company. The British, very keen to communicate directly with the natives and teach their young about European science and math, and have a mass-based vernacular for public communication, created Urdu for Muslims and Hindi for Hindus. Thus, from their very inception, both languages entered the public sphere with separate communal and cultural identities. As interest in Hindi grew and textbooks began to be printed swiftly and in large numbers, along with a rise in literacy, the politicisation of languages also began to rise. But unlike Europe, in India, the public sphere thus created was not made up of an increasingly self-confident bourgeoisie, but by a colonised public that followed many faiths and cultural practices and felt increasingly that its own essential cultural identity was under threat from 'modern' ideas. The public spheres that Hindi and Urdu went on to create in the vast Hindi heartland thus became ideal sites for politicians, creative writers and social reformers to display various interpretations of India's syncretic culture, mostly with a view to reconfirm or reshape prevalent political and socio-cultural ideas. As vernacular communication grew and began throwing up intellectual dissidents, the British government brought in the infamous Vernacular Press Act, 1878, that empowered it to jail writers and editors charged with seditious writings under the law and confiscate their press and other assets. This law was used copiously in the next century against many nationalist publications in Hindi, one of them being Gandhi's *Navjivan*, a Hindi weekly broadsheet published from Ahmedabad. When Gandhi was jailed, he began to bring out three dailies in Hindi, Gujarati and English. *Navjivan* was then re-named *Harijan*. It published editorials by Gandhi even when he was in jail and also serialised his famous *The Story of My Experiments with Truth* (1977 [1927]), translated into Hindi. In the late 1930s, Gandhi asked Nehru to start a trust and take the publication of his dailies in Hindi and English in hand. In 1938, the Associated Journals Ltd. was founded and went on to publish the Hindi *Navjivan*, the English *National Herald* and the Urdu *Quami Awaaz*. As the popular Urdu poet, Akbar Allahabadi (2009), wrote, '*Jab tope muquabil ho, akhbar nikalo!*' (When faced with a canon, launch a newspaper).

By the time India gained independence in 1947, the Hindi media had created a popular and large public space for itself, stamped with the Gandhian aura, and its acceptability among the nationalists in the northern states was high. But the very size of its footprint made Hindi suspect in many eyes. There were several ideologies that had come up in the first four decades of the twentieth century, which questioned the push that a section of the Hindi press seemed to be giving to communally divisive ideas. The succeeding period was marked by a clash of ideologies and a simultaneous push for deepening democratic ideals. This is where the real story of the Hindi print media begins.

2

Evolution of the Hindi Press
after Independence

*By 'the public sphere' we mean first of all a realm of our social
life in which something approaching public opinion can be
formed. Access is guaranteed to all citizens.*
Jürgen Habermas (1998; quoted in Jeffrey 2000: 11)

The expansion of the public sphere in India, unlike that in
Europe, has been neither uniform nor equal. It has a socio-
political history, where language choices are not made personally
but are driven by the caste, community and gender of the speaker.
This created fault-lines that were never eradicated, but were,
during the struggle for independence, buried deep within. In the
media, one major fault-line is where the colonial English language
plate collides with the vernacular mass and builds up energies that
rock the surface when they become too intense. English is still,
to most castes and classes denied English-medium education, a
symbol of colonial occupation and a marker of social inequality.
Of late, the politicisation of Hindi as a marker of Hindu identity
by India's Right-wing has revealed worrisome fault-lines between
India's vernacular media and the Hindi media that were lying
dormant. Within Hindi media today, one is witness to fault-lines
that run along Hindu and non-Hindu cultures, in particular,
Indo-Persian culture, and various dialects of Hindi, and the
government's version of a 'pure' (*shuddh*), Sanskritised Hindi, one
that is determined to purge itself of all 'foreign' words and fill
in the gaps with Sanskritic equivalents. The politicised part of

the Hindi press in India (like Vidyarthi's *Pratap* and Paradkar's *Aaj*) up until the 1940s had kept their prices low and expanded rapidly by emphasising their difference from the pricey English publications. They chose to give a voice to the political urges of the large Hindi-speaking public that the English dailies had failed to tap into. We cannot ignore, wrote Paradkar (1920), facts like the socio-economic class of our readers and the difficulties they face in their daily lives. If we wish to grow, we must give them information that they crave, in an easy-to-understand version of hybridised Hindi.

For their bitter parting of ways on communal grounds, both Hindi and Urdu have paid a heavy price. On 15 August 1947, when India made its tryst with destiny, eminent politicians from both sides of the Wagah border stood divided by political ideology, but both tacitly understood that the English language most leaders were educated in must remain the official language till contending claims from other regional languages against Hindi (in India) and Urdu (in Pakistan) had been settled as amicably as possible. Seventy years later, neither India nor Pakistan has been able to resolve this prickly issue and English remains the only official link language for both. In India, this has had important social and financial repercussions for Hindi, and indeed, all language journalism.

By the 1970s, many Indian journalists and creative writers in the north still considered writing in Hindi a political act, but as English became the language of power, Hindi bilingualism began to be discarded in the private school system. In most of the north, however, for political reasons, the vernacular as the medium of instruction was promoted vociferously by political leaders. But they began sending their own progeny to English-medium public schools. The majority of Indian families in the north were unable to afford private school education, and so, most of the neo-literates in the north read no English in school. The problem was that while the space for Hindi grew in the educational system, in practice, English continued to form the basic template for a successful career and upward social mobility. This helped retain the old caste/class divide, but produced large audiences for vernacular media.

Table 2.1:   Vernacular Dailies and Speakers in the
Early 1950s

Language	No. of dailies	Circulation (in thousands)	Population (in thousands)
Assamese	1	3	5,000
Bengali	7	240	25,100
Gujarati	23	187	16,300
Hindi	76	379	150,000
Kannada	25	72	14,500
Malayalam	21	196	13,400
Marathi	26	191	27,100
Oriya	3	43	12,200
Punjabi	9	23	-
Tamil	12	168	26,600
Telugu	6	98	33,000
Urdu	70	213	-
English	41	697	1,100

Source: Press Commission (1954: 26).

THE RISE OF HINDI PRINT IN INDIA IN THE EARLY 1970S

In the early 1970s, both editorials and their avid new readers experienced a unique roadblock in the expansion and mutation of the news business. The government, freshly bathed in the glory of the Bangladesh War and the dismembering of Pakistan, decided to add an additional tax of 15 per cent on imported newsprint. According to an editorial written by the then editor of *Nai Dunia* of Indore (Mathur 1992a [1971]), the pleadings of various newspaper barons and editors to reduce paper costs to enable them to sell their papers to literate but poor readers fell on deaf ears. It was felt that in the name of the poor, the rich owners and editors wanted to get concessions that would increase their own profit margins. The then finance minister, R. Venkataraman, said that he was a reader of the Chennai-based, popular English daily, *The Hindu*, the Mumbai-based *The Times of India* and the Delhi-based *Hindustan Times*. And he saw that all the papers carried a lot of advertising that reduced the space for news considerably, yet were still selling a 16–28 pager at a cost of 60–65 paise. They could certainly afford to pay the extra newsprint cost.

The question arose: What about the vernacular dailies that were read by the poor but had only 6–10 pages with little to no private advertising? No one asked this eminently sensible question. But other questions were posed, nevertheless: Can the government ration newsprint? Or decide the number of pages and/or the correct proportion of advertisements to news in an independent newspaper? If the newspapers are able to raise sufficient advertising from the market to sell their papers for free and still make a profit, will the government allow them to do so?

Soon, in 1972, the government came out with a newsprint policy that mandated that no paper should carry more than 10 pages, nor should newspapers be allowed to play with the number of pages for their outstation editions to beef up the main edition. Bennett, Colman and Company (also known as the Times Group) took the matter to the Supreme Court, which was already somewhat uneasy with the increasing assertion of power by the Central government over the judiciary. It rejected this policy.

The World of Hindi Print after 1977

After 1977, two factors changed newspapers and markets. The first was the swift rise of various Hindi-language periodicals edited by well-known Hindi poets and fiction writers. In Mumbai, Dharamvir Bharati created a new kind of weekly in Hindi with his *Dharmyug*, a Bennett, Colman and Company weekly that was aimed at the reading requirements of the typical Hindi-reading, middle-class family, not only in Delhi or Mumbai but also in various small towns and subdivisions across the Hindi belt. *Dharmyug* presented a mélange of essays about societal changes, the arts, major political happenings, with serialised fiction and poetry and literary criticism by eminent Hindi writers, along with cartoon strips and a page for children. Other major popular Hindi magazines with a similar mix were *Saptahik Hindustan* (from the *Hindustan Times* house) and *Dinman*. The latter was a weekly news magazine edited by Sachidanand Hiranand Vatsyayana, a well-known Hindi writer who trained his posse of writers to venture into Hindi reportage, and serious and informed political analysis. These magazines created professional infrastructures for Hindi within publishing houses and refined the tasks of reporting, editing and publishing stories from the vast Hindi heartland. These also revealed an India that lay beyond big cities and party headquarters. They were less well-produced than English weeklies like the *Illustrated Weekly of India*, but it was as though Hindi-speaking India had at last learnt to speak for itself. A decade later, major English weeklies also brought out Hindi weeklies. Thus, the *Hindi India Today*, *Ravivar* (from the Ananda Bazar Patrika Group of Kolkata), and last but not least, *Hindi Outlook* and *Tehelka*.

The second was after 1977, when India experimented with non-Congress governments. This new phase in politics was noticeable for its new crop of strong regional leaders from rural backgrounds, more at home with the vernaculars than English. This fact immediately created greater demand and widened the scope for vernacular newspapers to do in-depth political reporting, quoting leaders verbatim. Hindi newspapers and news magazines, exactly like their Tamil, Telugu, Kannada and Bangla counterparts, had already set out a fairly respectable arena for public discourse in Indian languages. And this space now included the humblest readers in remote small towns and villages, where the expansion of the school system was raising literacy rates steadily.

As the idea of inviolable freedom of speech once again became central and the middle class expanded some more, Brahminical Hindi, full of Sanskrit words and a certain pompous style of writing, began to give way to a more colloquial Hindi that happily accommodated Urdu, English, and the various north Indian variants of the official Khadi Boli. Editors and desks now realised the wisdom of Bharatendu, who had pointed out a century earlier that there could be no one-size-fits-all Hindi; that the north, from Punjab to Bihar, spoke in over a dozen variants of Hindi, liberally laced with local bolis (dialects) like Awadhi, Braj, Bhakha, Maithili and Bhojpuri, flecked with English, Persian and Portuguese words (see Shukla 1972).

Hindi Rises as a Clearing House for Vernacular Writing in India

An interesting feature of this period was that Hindi became a sort of clearing house for good writing in various Indian languages: Bangla, Tamil, Marathi, Punjabi, Malayalam, and so on. Three of the most popular Hindi magazines—*Dinman*, *Dharmyug* and *Saptahik Hindustan*—introduced countless small-town readers to the writings of Ismat Chughtai, S. L. Bhyrappa, U. R. Ananthamurthy, Badal Sarkar, Vijay Tendulkar, and many others. All these magazines, edited by eminent Hindi writers—Agyeya, Shrikant Verma, Dharamvir Bharati and Manohar Shyam Joshi—were cross-subsidised for decades by the revenues incurred from the house English and Hindi dailies. With the closure of magazines, this very valuable space fast atrophied.

In 1978, Rajendra Mathur (1992b [1978]) wrote despairingly in an editorial how the daily circulation of any Hindi paper was yet to touch the magic figure of a million. This, despite the fact that the total copies sold by the 4,196 Hindi newspapers had touched 9.7 million, and had left English newspapers (a total of 15,800) behind, with only nine million copies being sold in toto. Still, by the end of the decade, there was unmistakable growth, both in the numbers and sales figures of Hindi print media. A report by the registrar of newspapers that was placed before the Parliament in 1979 recorded that in 1978 alone, Hindi papers had recorded a growth of 11.8 per cent. By now, Hindi dailies numbered 318. It also highlighted an interesting trend in the ownership of major dailies, including Hindi. Twenty-five major units, that by now owned almost 17 per cent of the total circulation of Indian dailies, were closely related to big businesses other than publishing and reflected common economic and political interests and opinions.

The 1980s: Change Becomes More Visible

The politically volatile 1980s may not have improved revenues substantially, but the years did bring Hindi media practitioners personally and collectively closer to various dominant political ideologies and regional leaders in the Hindi belt. Various major politicians heading non-Congress parties: Ram Manohar Lohia, Jayaprakash Narayan, Janeshwar Mishra, Madhu Limaye, George Fernandes, etc., were also votaries of Indian languages. The Hindi journalists, editors and media barons were no longer seen by them as adversaries or messengers for political leaders from the ruling Congress, but as the sort of communicators they needed to reach out to the masses. Many journalists and editors became close confidants of political leaders and carried out socio-political depth soundings for them from time to time. Several were even nominated to the Upper House of Parliament. An example of this was Shrikant Verma, an erstwhile senior editor with the Times Group's Hindi news weekly, *Dinman*, who rose to be Indira Gandhi's media advisor and was nominated to the Rajya Sabha. His colleagues, like Sarveshwar Dayal Saxena and Raghuvir Sahay, became ardent supporters of other eminent politicians, like socialist leader Lohia, a known baiter of Indira Gandhi, Mishra, and among the Congressmen, V. P. Singh, Janardan Dwivedi, Sudhakar Dwivedi, Arjun Singh and Shyama Charan Shukla.

Rajiv Gandhi's sudden arrival coincided with the period when a vast number of neo-literate readers/voters in the small-town and rural Hindi heartland became upwardly mobile. With Rajiv talking animatedly of bringing in computers and opening up the markets to investors, aspirations were rising. The richer farmers were now keen to send their sons to larger towns to enter the newly opened institutes of higher education and technology or appear for the civil services entrance exams. The younger readers from villages and smaller towns were looking around for vernacular papers and periodicals that would help expand their mental horizons and crack the admission exams. They were willing to spend good money to buy their periodicals, and tea shops, coffee houses and college debating were becoming active hubs for young minds, where people shared their newspapers and periodicals and hotly debated various political and social issues long into the night.

In the early 1980s, among the 28 highest selling Indian dailies, four were in Hindi: *Navbharat Times* (Delhi), *Hindustan* (Delhi), *Punjab Kesari* (Jalandhar) and *Nai Dunia* (Indore). By the mid-1980s, the steady rise of an ambitious, young, Hindi-speaking middle class in the vast Hindi belt had firmly debunked the myth that Hindi readers were too poor to afford vernacular language dailies and periodicals. Bihar and Uttar Pradesh, two of the poorest states in India's Hindi belt, emerged as the biggest buyers of Hindi print. A sudden 40 per cent jump was recorded in the circulation of Hindi dailies. Already in 1978, the first National Readership Survey (NRS) had reported that the vernacular papers, particularly Hindi, had come to command a vast readership that was several times the readership of their English counterparts (IMRB and ORG 1978). The gap between English and Hindi dailies kept widening. And more Hindi readers began buying their own copies instead of sharing a copy with many others.

Table 2.2: Rise in Literacy, 1951–2011

Year	Male (per cent)	Female (per cent)	Combined (per cent)
1951	27.16	8.86	18.33
1961	40.4	15.35	28.3
1971	45.96	21.97	34.45
1981	56.38	29.76	43.57
1991	64.13	39.29	52.21
2001	75.26	53.67	64.83
2011	82.14	65.46	74.04

Source: RGCCI (2016).

THE STRANGE INDIAN AMBIVALENCE TO ADVERTISING

Gandhi, as editor, remained firmly opposed to accepting advertising for his publications. He preferred crowdfunding and philanthropic support instead. Many private newspaper houses like Tilak's *Hind Kesari* accepted ads at the rate of four annas (Rs 0.25) per line, and if the bookings extended to a year, the rate for one inch of column space was Rs 12 per annum. Periodicals like *Chaand*, *Madhuri* and *Didi* also accepted advertising. Gandhi's successor, Nehru, with his socialist leanings, was also sceptical of advertising, which he believed could lead the revenue-givers into manipulating newspapers and their owners.

At this point, ironically, most advertising came from the government. And until proprietors of Hindi papers that rose to great prominence in the next few decades, like the Varanasi-based *Aaj* (1920), Kanpur-based *Dainik Jagran* (1947) and Agra-based *Amar Ujala* (1948), actively solicited government advertising from state governments, the bulk of government advertising continued to be allocated to English-language papers, which, despite their smaller circulation figures, were classed as 'national'. Despite loud disclaimers from the Directorate of Advertising and Visual Publicity (DAVP), the release or holding back of advertising by governments to reward or punish newspapers has since been a common feature all over India. As the growth spurt began in the mid-1970s, the revenue from the cover price was unable to cover the fast-rising costs of publishing, and of buying and installing new machinery at various print locations in the Hindi belt. Initially, privately generated advertising revenues for Hindi papers accrued from what was termed as 'classified advertising'. These small ads for various consumer goods and services were printed in smaller fonts and bunched together in what was referred to as the 'classified pages'. The largest ads in this genre were matrimonials, and larger papers had them in sufficient numbers so as to create special weekend pages, and later, whole pull-outs. By the mid-1980s, classified ads for jobs also grew sufficiently, so as to merit a weekly 'employment' pull-out. These were so popular that on Thursdays, when the Hindi papers usually brought out the pull-outs on jobs and student tutorials, sales registered an unmistakable upward swing. In the marketplace (Hindi papers being mostly sold from stalls), stall owners placed these weekly pull-outs on top of the main papers, so buyers could compare the proffered ads and choose the paper that suited their requirements the most.

THE FIRST READERSHIP SURVEYS CARRIED OUT BY MULTINATIONALS

With the growth of the middle classes, revisions in salaries of government servants and banks offering loans for buying homes, the classifieds also saw a jump in pull-outs for real estate. Consumer non-durables, such as soaps, balms, hair oils and edible oils, also became major and regular contributors of advertising in Hindi dailies. It was Hindustan Unilever that carried out the first in-depth readership survey, followed by Dabur. Both surveys proved conclusively that the Hindi belt offered the largest markets for building up consumer bases through customised advertising. The high numbers of new consumers soon alerted Indian advertising agencies, which had thus far treated Hindi papers as downmarket products unfit for advertising goods in. After the initial hiccups, the liberalisation of the Indian economy led, in the 1990s, to a rise in the expenditure on advertising in the language media by all major companies, both national and international. Egged on by market research that revealed that localisation could open doors to a vast new readership of people living in rural areas and smaller towns, the bigger dailies began bringing out numerous local editions with the help of digital technology and stringers, and expanding printing facilities into towns close to these areas.

How the 1990s Began to Change Revenue Structures within the Print Industry

Sometime around the late 1990s, some major English dailies decided to reduce the per copy cost of newspapers to drastically to drive out their rivals from the fast-filling market, and simultaneously go all out to garner more and more ad revenues to cross-subsidise printing costs and make bigger profits. They introduced the devilishly cunning scheme of offering advertisements, or advertorials disguised as news, for a good price. A new genre, cleverly labelled as 'ad for equity', also came up. The philosophy underlying this was that the newspaper was not an embodiment of certain long-standing values and traditions, but a commercial product, and what the new, young reader wants to read is visually exciting articles about celebrities, about smart, prêt clothing and designer goods and eateries. But if you do specific write-ups on certain brands and restaurants, they will earn more. So subsidiaries were set up and anybody who wished to be featured in the newspapers had to pay for the space. With these measures, mainstream media in Hindi also began to print promotional articles about individuals, products and corporate houses for a fee, brazenly disguising the pieces as news stories. This was met with loud applause from bosses all round.

Hindi dailies again followed their English counterparts, with feature pull-outs of slightly more affordable versions of places and people to look out for. To the smart, whiz-kid managers employed by publishers of Hindi dailies and periodicals, reinventing print media as a lucrative multi-language, multi-edition business became a major preoccupation. The small-town market, by and large an autonomous phenomenon but somewhat constrained by politics, invented its own localised versions.

The Story of Vijay Singh's Life: From Hawker to Marketing Manager

To me, the story of Vijay Singh's life, as he rose from a newspaper hawker to being the national head of the Hindustan Times Group, is a microcosm of the world that Hindi newspapers had created in the 1980s. His Hindi autobiography, *Hawker se haakim* (From Hawker to Officer; 2018), unfolds the story of the growth of India's Hindi print media and the changes it experienced over the years.

Singh began as a hawker for the Calcutta-based Statesman group in Patna, in the undivided state of Bihar, when the news business was picking up. He was one of the many young and poor students who became part-time hawkers to supplement their income and pay their fees. Owners used them to sell their papers piecemeal by the wayside, in the markets and railway stations. They were poorly paid and the hours were long, but being good at his job, in 1980, Singh was handpicked by the Searchlight-Pradip group, a powerful local house that published a Hindi and an English paper.

Having bagged a much sought-after post as an agent, who received 60 per cent per copy sold, he now had a chance to build his own team of hawkers and was reimbursed in full for copies that remained unsold. In the vast state of Bihar, the major news agents ruled the scene. Newspapers and periodicals were variously distributed by state-run buses, trains, even steamers and taxis, to tap far-off rural markets that were developing a new generation of Hindi papers and periodicals. When floods came, the teams of hawkers donned mackintoshes, and armed with torches, crossed rivers in steamers to distribute papers in villages that stood on the other side.

By 1981, the better agents had mutated into mega agents who would do anything to protect their precious precincts. This included fighting pitched battles against rivals with hired musclemen and family members, and using local MLAs to provide political cover. The agent *babus* (bureaucrats) controlled the hawkers' unions. And at their behest, these unions organised a memorable strike against the Searchlight group, when they wanted to hand over part of their distribution system to a rival. The communal rioting in 1981 also played a role here. When the curfew paralysed the streets in Bihar, Singh organised 22 boot-polish boys at the Patna station. He paid them several times what they earned as boot polishers and got them hawking their wares as 'his' men. Overnight, the paper business picked up and Singh, the agent, had arrived! As his fame spread, in 1984, when the powerful Leader Press of Allahabad wished to sack a marketing manager who had turned rogue, Singh and his team were sent for. The matter, Singh (2018: 47) writes, was soon resolved and the unwanted bully evicted from the company house and press premises.

In 1986, the Delhi-based K. K. Birla, the son of G. D. Birla, decided to launch the Hindi *Hindustan* and English *Hindustan Times* in Patna. At that point, printing, bundling and distribution were all done manually and needed seasoned teams like Singh's, who understood the intricacies and occasional use of the fabled *jugaad* practices (indigenous approaches of getting results through locally and easily available material). Apart from handling the bundling and routine distribution, the agent could also utilise vital local networks of vendors, goons and MLAs, if need be. When the *Hindustan Times* bought out the Searchlight-Pradip group along with its entire team of dedicated and seasoned workers, Singh joined the Hindustan Times Group that he was to spend the next three decades with. The English *Hindustan Times* and Hindi *Hindustan* papers were successfully launched. And for the next three decades, the Hindi *Hindustan* ruled the roost.

THE FLAMBOYANT PLAYERS OF THE 1990S

By 1993, writes Singh (2018: 68–69), a new player had arrived in town—the charismatic Subrata Roy, also known as Sahara Shree. A

Great Gatsby-like flamboyant figure, who started life as a railway clerk, and then went on to launch a very successful chit fund scheme and then the Sahara group of airlines, the tagline of which read, 'Emotionally yours'. He brought his Hindi paper, *Sahara*, to Patna, accompanied by a posse of smooth-talking, sophisticated marketing managers. Aware that the vendors formed the backbone of the distribution system in the Hindi market, the Sahara group introduced what were referred to as very attractive 'schemes' for both vendors and readers. These included a bicycle for each vendor who sold 20 copies and a motorbike for selling 200 copies. They offered annual bookings at negligible rates to readers with various kinds of gifts. Some vendors and marketing agents who had performed well were rewarded by being flown in the company's planes to Delhi to meet Sahara Shree face to face.

After a few years' dream run, the Sahara group got involved in prolonged litigation on charges of launching what seemed like a Ponzi scheme, and this very interesting paper that gave the Hindi media a run for its money till the mid-1990s petered out. The last decade of the twentieth century saw the unimaginable expansion of Hindi dailies, localisation of content through myriad editions and the extensive use of new technology that made it possible to bring out district editions through inexpensively housed and furnished rural modem centres that mopped up all the local news and advertising and then sent the ready-to-print local page to the nearest print location for an editorial once-over, printing and distribution.

The simultaneous bifurcation of the Hindi states of Bihar, Madhya Pradesh and Uttar Pradesh once again ignited intense territorial wars. *Prabhat Khabar*, a Ranchi-based paper, controlled the local hawkers' union firmly and beat back most rivals. It had actively participated in the political haggling to separate the mineral-rich state of Jharkhand from Bihar, and won a deeply devout following among the locals and the tribals alike. In 2000, *Dainik Jagran*, with deeper pockets and more political clout, took it on. *Prabhat Khabar* still remains one of the best produced and respected dailies in the area.

By now, all major publishing houses—the Times Group, the Hindustan Times, Mitra Prakashan (Allahabad), Ananda Bazar Patrika, and the Dilli Press—were seized with a fever to start regional editions for their papers. But the agents were a very powerful lobby who acted as a bottleneck. Still, the Hindi dailies went on a localisation spree, often using franchisees, who, for a certain agreed-upon amount, provided the land, the printing press and the machines. They distributed the papers early by using fleets of taxis.

The Subrata Roy-led Sahara had generated several successful rewards and special schemes to attract numbers. This practice was soon picked up by rival papers. *Hindustan* launched a lottery-like scheme, whereby a lucky buyer would be selected on the basis of a computer-generated lottery number to receive a Maruti car. When one winner was abducted by dacoits, who demanded that the management hand them the car since they had 'convinced' the actual winner that he would be happier with the motorcycle they gave him, and again, after a computer operator demanded a 'cut' from another winner, whose father, being a high official, raised a stink, this scheme was dropped and replaced with a new 'scratch and win' scheme.

NEW OWNERSHIP STRUCTURES AND THE BEGINNING OF MEDIA MONOPOLIES

The ownership system that had emerged in Hindi publishing with the princely houses was followed by freedom fighters who doubled up as owners-cum-printers in the mould of their idols Gandhi, Tilak and Malaviya—all owner-editors. They were followed by new entrepreneurs from smaller towns, who launched papers that became quite eminent and locally celebrated over the years. Some of these were *Jagran* (Kanpur 1947), *Dainik Bhaskar* (Bhopal 1958), *Amar Ujala* (Agra 1948), *Navbharat Times* (Mumbai 1950), *Nai Dunia* (Indore 1947), *Rajasthan Patrika* (Jaipur 1956), *Punjab Kesari* (Jalandhar 1966), *Jansatta* (Delhi 1983) and *Rashtriya Sahara* (Delhi 1998).

Ownership of Hindi media in India differs from Europe in that media oligarchs there are usually people well-trained and experienced in media. In India, successful vernacular media by the 1980s had come to be run by businessmen, whose primary interests were in other sectors of industry, with their media businesses being only a useful door-opener to power politics. After the insurance and banking sectors were nationalised by the late 1970s, the media barons acquired interests in these sectors as well. In the north, many major media houses have gained positions in the company boards of various sugar, cotton, cement, textile and chemical manufacturing companies as major investors. Just as the technological shift from the lithograph to Linotype and Monotype machines created a mass market for the printed word in the early twentieth century, the easing of rules for importing newsprint and the latest technology (offset presses and computer-based typesetting and composing) made publishing a very attractive commercial proposition for Indian capitalists. Indian companies in the post-liberalisation period began manufacturing offset presses, which, as Robin Jeffrey (2000: 39–40) says, 'became a workhorse of Indian newspapers'.

A few major houses eventually were able to own the media, both horizontally (in terms of content creation) and vertically (in terms of distribution). Many Hindi papers such as *Jagran*, *Punjab Kesari*, *Nai Dunia* and *Dainik Bhaskar* have owners presiding over them as super editors; all have launched their e-papers and many of them, successful news portals as well. Most have inherited their positions in the media houses, established by their fathers or grandfathers. They may, in time, give up some of the equity shares to others but continue to impact the shape of their publications as the declared or undeclared chief editor. Since the pressure of raising funds and dealing with corporate and HR issues exerts huge pressure to publish or withhold certain kinds of news, or format it in a way that suits the funding agencies, several recent steps for redefining news suggest they were taken after bypassing the editorials.

The Rise of Managers and the Denting of Editorial Firewalls

By the end of the twentieth century, hardcore editorial work, that involves constant checking and verification of facts, investigating wrongdoing at the higher levels of power hierarchies and getting the version from the other side so the story is well-rounded, had become somewhat diluted under pressure from the boardrooms. The editor, already under pressure from the owners, became answerable on a day-to-day basis to the managers, whose job it was to keep the system going and protect the multiple business interests of the owners. The nomination of several owners/editors to the Upper House of

Parliament meant that their papers would become promoters of the political parties that nominated them. Initially, some senior editors and media bodies expressed deep concern over such a dilution of their professional work, but the new structure proved to be difficult to demolish in its entirety.

According to the veteran journalist Chandan Mitra (2006), it is not the politicisation of editors but the progressive reduction in the price of newspapers that lies at the core of the debasing of public taste. Most readers have no idea what it actually costs to print and publish a newspaper, which they buy at a much lower price thanks to its cross-subsidisation by advertisers. Such low-cost newspapers exist only in India, where the entire economics of newspapers has been distorted by the predatory circulation tactics of certain major dailies, followed by the opening of floodgates to advertising that masquerades as news. Advertisers in India are still looking at the quantity of readership, rather than the quality. Newspapers with a proven, large circulatory base can command the biggest advertising accounts.

But here we notice another discrepancy. Vernacular, in particular Hindi, newspapers, despite having a circulation base several times that of the local English-language dailies, unless they are number one, still attract less revenue. The advertising world is still not persuaded that a Hindi newspaper reader can spend as much as one who reads an English paper. After the global market's sudden and unforeseen meltdown, there was a spell when the realty, aviation and automobile sectors went into a tailspin one after another, and companies that adopted schemes to distribute freebies to readers, vendors and news agents were left red-faced and holding bags of (economy class) air tickets, empty flats and unsold cars. Elections, however, were near, so plentiful political advertising and exit polls financed by interested groups helped compensate for the losses to a large extent.

THE GROWTH OF POLITICAL ADVERTISING IN HINDI

The dailies may or may not have collected their crores with duplicitous exercises in psephology, but a new idea of what has now come to be called 'political advertising' was planted across the country, triggering off another lucrative trend. Soon, the marketing and media marketing managers at several media houses were getting 'creatives' prepared about what was on offer. Several party functionaries who had manned the party 'war rooms' during the period, when quizzed, confessed to having been shown several 'impressive' PowerPoint presentations by major newspapers, and in turn, professing an interest in the offerings.

A hard copy of one such offering, made on behalf of a Hindi daily published from a rich western state, blatantly delineates the phenomena. The script claims that some 36 Lok Sabha seats in two major cities in the state, including the state capital and surrounding areas, were 'feeded' (*sic*) by the said daily. The proposal then lays down a clear, sequential map of activities it can spearhead for promoting the party or individual candidates, quoting clear prices. At the local level, it addresses the candidate, supporters/well-wishers, the district-level party office, the local MLA/MLC/corporators, local political leaders, the local advertising agency and the guardian minister of the ruling party. At the state level, it addresses the state political party office, state cabinet ministers and state-level political leaders, businessmen/industrialists and the state-level advertising agency. At the apex (national) level, it addresses the central offices of political parties (media cells), national-level political leaders and central cabinet ministers belonging to the state.

Today, as our vernacular media readers are getting younger and more volatile and more demanding, they are most likely in small towns, where an elegant bank with an ATM stands in the middle of shanties and huts with TV antennae. Here, after leaving the railway station or the airport, one almost always plunges into the darkness of a grim, squalid road full of potholes, and in the marketplace, besides the glittering shop windows with Dior watches and Mont Blanc pens, the unlit windows of local shops lie empty and unlit. Private capital, that has arrived in small towns piggybacking on the Hindi dailies, has only constructed shining sanctuaries for the rich. To read many marketing-driven Hindi dailies today is increasingly like entering a tumultous zone where endless, fierce and frantic discussions continue over everything, from Beijing's beastliness to Bt brinjal and Raj Babbar, to cloyingly hagiographic accounts of how Rahul *Baba* alone led his party to triumph in the recent by-polls. Actually, there are too many people now in the media industry whose answer to the question, 'What is the media for?' is, 'To make money.'

Certainly there is nothing wrong in restructuring the industry and making it more productive, more vibrant. The Janata Party government began the process and the BJP and the Congress have continued to support this. The government-controlled audio-visual media was certainly too big and lumbering and arrogant, and was easily pushed to the margins by the leaner and more efficient private players. But why has the hugely successful Hindi print media, which has always been in private hands and quite free professionally, begun to trivialise their own base and con their readership for piffling, short-term gains? If this trend continues, the readers will react and the next round of closures will have more serious implications, not only for those who will lose their jobs, but also for the readers' understanding of where they live and how their reality is inviolable and a part of the nation's.

As professionals, we find this a worrying trend. But fortunately, this is not sustainable in the long run. If one looks at the number of TV channels and Hindi papers, and how the young in the north are getting their news, one realises that they are less and less interested in newspapers, except when they are preparing for a civil services exam or a quiz contest. If you want just headlines and 300-word copy, you can read on your mobile screen anywhere, at whatever time. The core newspaper readers in Hindi are no longer kids in a candy store. If they want consumer goods-related information, they can download it on the mobiles they carry around all the time. The 1990s' formula is dying, and slowly but surely, the newspaper market is shifting towards digital platforms.

The indications are clear. Those who will stick to newspapers will be the people who want to read, so there will be newspapers with limited circulation, purged of much of the trivia they have been dishing out, and with more food for thought and more verified information about life and politics and civic issues. And they would not mind paying more for professionally produced newspapers, thus cutting down on their fatal dependency on advertisers.

CONCLUSION

When India became independent, the big question on both sides of the border was: Which among the multiple regional vernaculars should be India's and Pakistan's national language? Gandhi's suggestion favoured Hindi for India, and Jinnah saw Urdu as the real peoples' language for the Pakistanis. But both Hindi and Urdu were firmly rejected as national languages by speakers of other native vernaculars, both in India and in Pakistan. So after 73 years, English continues to be an official language. English dailies command far smaller readership than vernacular dailies and digital media, yet English is used as the link language. Most English papers had modelled themselves along the lines of popular British dailies. And Hindi dailies, though they commanded much larger readership across the vast Hindi belt, remained starved of advertising revenues. The pattern still continues with digital news platforms, which use technology, keyboards and fonts created for Western clients, most of them familiar with the English language.

The revenue models, however, have undergone a sea change after the 1970s. Earlier, Hindi dailies brought out by big publishing houses had sister English dailies that were cash rich. They mostly cross-subsidised the vernacular dailies and magazines. Most smaller regional Hindi papers had to work within exceedingly small budgets and could only afford indigenous newsprint and old-style print technology. Things began to change in the latter half of the 1970s, and the reasons were both political and social. In 1975, after the dreaded Emergency that had clamped down on the media was lifted and a new coalition with many powerful leaders from the Hindi heartland replaced Indira Gandhi's party at the Centre, the vernaculars, especially Hindi, became an important tool of public communication for the new power pack. In 1978, the first National Readership Survey reflected this huge growth in the number of Hindi readers, which far outstripped that of English media. This was also a point when media barons, like the late Ramnath Goenka of *The Indian Express*, became very closely identified with India's emerging power equations, with editors like Arun Shourie who, with the owner's backing, were willing to speak truth to power, no matter what the cost. Several Hindi editors (most of them editing magazines for the Times Group) also interacted closely with the Congress and the socialists as their sounding boards and unofficial advisors. Even after the Congress came back to power, the close relationship between Hindi editors and political parties continued, which was to have far-reaching consequences in the coming decades.

The ambivalence towards advertising in the Indian system, however, took another two decades to dissolve. The 1990s introduced Hindi daily owners to the power of mergers. The mega Hindi dailies now entered regional markets other than the ones they had dominated so far, buying up smaller local papers to help inflate numbers and localise news for their new regional editions. Simultaneously, a different revenue model was crafted for advertising in Hindi print. Growing numbers and ad revenues sharpened the competition in the Hindi market and brought in flamboyant figures like the Sahara group's Sahara Shree, whose papers aggressively pushed their way into various regional markets and launched attractive 'schemes' and rewards for enhancing readership subscriptions. The autobiography of Vijay Singh, *Hawker se haakim* (2018), clearly maps out this extremely interesting and fast-paced era, where everything, from schemes to musclemen and gun-toting goons, were used to disband rival hawkers' unions and send lesser competitors scurrying. By the end of the century, all this created a market and readership for Hindi that was unique, vast and bullish.

3

How the Hindi Newspaper Business Changed

It is a truth universally acknowledged in the market that readership data is the basic currency used to buy and sell media space. Seventy per cent of the media's revenues are earned thus. But until the early 1990s, when anecdotal wisdom, not hard data, drove the game, India was a very different place for the Hindi media. In my long career as an editor, I handled various monthly and weekly Hindi magazines and the multi-edition Hindi daily, *Hindustan*, for two of India's biggest media houses. All through, I heard various chiefs of marketing tell me that I should excuse them for not reading the 'product' themselves, as they did not read Hindi. But, they were always quick to add, they regularly checked with their barber, driver, *ayah* (nanny), *khansama* (waiter or cook) or house guard, and when asked, all of them said that it was a good read. The marketing managers also agreed that their ideal reader was not a 'person like us'. It was someone who read Hindi only because they could not read English. Two well-known owners confided that they had deliberately chosen to retain their successful English publications' name for their Hindi product, as it gave them an upmarket image in the English-crazy Hindi heartland. One of them told me that the aspirational small-town Hindi reader today must love to win friends and influence people among those they saw as having 'arrived'. So by quoting the name of this Hindi magazine when talking about their reading habits, one could easily lure people into believing that the magazine being named was the English version.

By the late 1980s, from TV sets to denim jeans, the most coveted items for personal consumption for India's upwardly mobile, urban middle classes were the imported ones. As 'mind products', in the new manager-ese fast becoming popular, Hindi newspapers and periodicals, even though they were registering vast sales, were considered somewhat lowbrow. Hindi print media was, to the upper-middle-class India to which most young owners, ad agency executives and managers of major publishing houses belonged, something consumed by a low visibility, high financial risk universe: clerks, drivers, small shop owners, nannies, *dhaba-wallahs* (people who run wayside eateries) and housewives. When they fanned out to agencies offering space for ads, they basically promoted the house English dailies and threw in a special offer in the shape of a simultaneous placement of the ad in the Hindi daily for almost half the price. Indeed, some of them felt truly mortified by the prospect of handling a Hindi product. Around the year 2000, at a group promotional function, the then marketing manager, I was told, did not wish to be photographed with the lower-grade marketing staff of the Hindi paper for fear of tainting her image as a smart, young marketing manager among her colleagues, and downgrading her worth in the market.

THE CUNNING PASSAGES AND WHISPERING CORRIDORS OF THE HINDI BELT

The Indian markets in the Hindi belt have harboured within them age-old cunning passages and whispering corridors. Brilliant young editors were men (myself being the sole exception, more or less): S. P. Singh of the Ananda Bazar Patrika Group driving a news weekly, *Ravivar*, Prabhu Chawla of the Hindi *India Today*, Manohar Shyam Joshi of the Hindustan Times Group's weekly, *Saptahik Hindustan*, Rajendra Mathur, editor of the Times Group's Hindi *Navbharat Times*, Prabhash Joshi, who launched the Hindi *Jansatta* for the Express group, and scores of others dotted the field. They were never given their due until some of them began appearing on TV and became overnight celebrities in the field of news analysis and debate. But still, a glaring lack of proper staff and in-depth coverage of financial and corporate issues caused distortions in business reporting in Hindi and continues to this day.

The social snobberies of the managers and space sellers of Hindi media did not allow them to see how serious business opportunities had been slowly developing in the last two decades of the twentieth century in Tier 2 cities like Kanpur, Jalandhar, Jaipur, Pune, Nagpur and Raipur. Local business reporters, being largely absent, and the visible or invisible pressures on editors (and/or direct orders to bureau representatives from the managers/owners) to keep major sources of corporate and political advertising happy, often led to slanted interpretations, inaccuracies or plain untruths with no clear mention of sources. This was the time of the business boom of the mid-1990s, when IPOs (Initial Public Offerings) were increasing and verifiable business news were badly needed in Hindi among average, middle-class Hindi media consumers. But most CEOs and ad managers in mega publishing houses continued to strategise about how to attract more readers for their English dailies and cut costs for the Hindi dailies, which they were reluctant to promote despite visible proof that colour TVs, soft drinks, and all manner of white goods were being bought by the middle classes in small-town India and the rural rich in villages.

Gradually, the ambivalence of the Hindi print media towards advertising (based initially on a Gandhian worldview and later on class bias) was discarded. Around the mid-1990s, the larger sales figures of Hindi papers began to be too visible to ignore. As a matter of fact, the annual Indian Readership Surveys were also throwing up figures showing that in each part of India, vernacular print media was far outselling English, and stirrings finally began in the usually placid world of owners and managers. The capitalised billings for Hindi rose by over 30 per cent by 1998 (MRUC 2019b).

Two years later as the new millennium arrived, the advertisers' worldview underwent a total sea change. In 2001, India's decadal census highlighted a dramatic growth in literacy rates in the country. Among the most backward northern 'BIMARU' (Bihar, Madhya Pradesh, Rajasthan and Uttar Pradesh) states in the Hindi belt, Madhya Pradesh and Chhattisgarh (included in this grouping after its formation) registered almost a one-fifth decline in illiteracy within a decade and in Rajasthan, literacy rates jumped by over 22 per cent, when the national average for rise in literacy for the same period was a little above 13 per cent (RGCCI 2001). Television, first seen as an enemy, had proved to be a great friend of the print media, in that it made people more eager to read newspapers and extend and verify information. According to the annual National Readership Survey, there were 131 million readers for Hindi print in 1999. By 2002, their numbers had grown to 155 million, and by 2005, to 200 million (Ninan 2007: 15). So here was incontrovertible proof that by the new millennium, when the West faced a fast shrivelling of its print media, India had emerged as the largest publisher of print in the world with close to 6,700 publications and over 260 million copies distributed daily.

A New Success Story Gets Written

According to the Indian Readership Survey (IRS) report released in the last week of April 2019, more than 425 million readers read a newspaper in the first quarter of 2019, as against 407 million in the first quarter of 2017 (MRUC 2019a). The Audit Bureau of Circulations (ABC) data of 2016 has already shown that with an average growth of 4.87 per cent per annum, India's media industry is one of the biggest growth stories in the early twenty-first century. Actually, the Cinderella story of India's vernacular media, particularly the Hindi media, began to take shape between 2002 and 2005. Readership in UP, Bihar and Jharkhand at that point saw phenomenal annual growth of 14 per cent, with over two-thirds of these readers based in small towns and rural areas (ABC 2016). Despite the continuous political turbulence, poverty, rise in crime and near breakdown of law and order, or perhaps because of them, poor but news-hungry readers in Bihar and Jharkhand were ready to spend Rs 5 per copy for a slim Hindi newspaper, almost three times the per-copy price of the (several times fatter) major English dailies.

According to Round 1 of the IRS 2009, the list of India's top 10 dailies contained only Indian language newspapers, of which six were in Hindi. India's largest English daily, *The Times of India*, stood outside the 'Big Ten', at number 11. And according to the IRS 2008 (Round 2), its total sales (13.34 million copies per day) were but a fraction of the vast numbers sold by the top four Hindi dailies in the list: *Dainik Jagran* (55.74 million), *Dainik Bhaskar* (33.83

million), *Amar Ujala* (29.38 million) and *Hindustan* (26.63 million) (Pande 2009b).

THE SLOW MORPHING OF THE HINDI EDITOR INTO AN ACTIVE PARTICIPANT IN POLITICS

When the humongous growth in readership and the hunger for more news made it necessary to employ more, and create functional bureaus and city desks, an unspoken problem in Hindi once again came to the fore: How to attend to editors who would not just edit but also be politically astute enough to influence the ruling political cliques?

In the earliest days, Hindi editors and editorial staff were employed on the basis of word of mouth. The blue-blooded owners of Hindi papers seldom, if ever, read Hindi, much less interacted closely with those who spoke it. When Raja Rampal Singh of Kalakankar, for example, needed an editor for his Hindi paper, he asked around at Benares College and was suggested the name of a bright but poor student, Madan Mohan Malaviya, who was then studying law. When Raja Shiv Prasad 'Sitara e Hind' similarly needed an editor for his Varanasi-based paper, he consulted Malaviya, who asked them to recruit an editor from the campus of the Haridwar-based Gurukul Kangri, one of the few colleges that taught Hindi and dispensed degrees of Vidyalankar upon graduation. Many of the earliest Hindi editors thus arrived with Vidyalankar as their second name (including the first editor of *Dharmyug*, Satyakam Vidyalankar, and Bhimsen Vidyalankar, editor of Lok Seva Mandal of Lala Lajpat Rai). There were exceptions, of course, like the fiery Ganesh Shankar Vidyarthi of Kanpur, who died trying to save Muslims from being killed during the riots in 1947, or the Marathi Brahmin, Baburao Vishnu Paradkar of Varanasi. But they were exceptions, not the rule. The average Hindi editor remained a paid employee, recruited more on the basis of his caste or on the recommendation of some trusted friend or political heavyweight. The owners, many of whom were keen to launch a Hindi daily to expand their other businesses and acquire political muscle, mostly obliged. By the 1990s, political backing for an incumbent began to emerge as a major factor for selecting editors of Hindi dailies. Most owners of Hindi dailies were traders-turned-capitalists. Their businesses were mostly family-owned and family-run. When the patriarch retired or passed away, genetic roulette decided who among the heirs would head leadership positions in the financial, legal, technical or the human resource divisions. They stayed together and played the game by the traditional rules set by the founding fathers.

Most houses that published both an English daily and another in Hindi used somewhat different criteria when picking an editor for their English or vernacular publication. The editors from English dailies were mostly from upper-middle-class families and had easy access to bureaucrats and politicians who read only English dailies that were respectfully referred to as 'national'. Even after the political dispensation became heavy with vernacular-speaking stalwarts like K. Kamaraj, J. Jayalalitha, Chandra Shekhar, Atal Bihari Vajpayee, the feisty triad of Lalu Prasad Yadav, Mulayam Singh Yadav and Mayawati, and Janeshwar Mishra and Nitish Kumar, the bureaucracy who briefed them and conducted the pressers showed an obvious bias against the vernacular press, perhaps unconsciously. The vernacular-speaking political leaders preferred to recommend names and positions for the vernacular publications that they read carefully each day. Some astute ministers who headed the Ministry of Information and Broadcasting at the Central level seeded the desks of Hindi publications with young party acolytes, who, as senior sub-editors or news editors, proved to be a great help to the party a few years down the line. Every Hindi editor was aware of this, and also the political predilections of the embedded employees, who could only be transferred but not sacked.

The concept of consciously enlightening students of journalism about some of the above grim facts or the early flawed marketing of Hindi print products has been largely absent in our books on journalism. But these facts have played a spectacular role in the political partisanship that the major Hindi dailies have displayed at critical moments in our national history. Courses in both journalism and marketing remain bewilderingly English-oriented, where the sharp *desi* (local) insights of senior managers of successful Hindi publications in highly competitive markets have mostly gone unnoticed. It is a pity, because the attitude of media managers and marketing departments in publishing houses with multi-media products on offer might often use a one-size-fits-all technique for selling ad space or marketing Hindi dailies. It is time that students of journalism looked at houses that focused on a single Hindi product and rose to be market leaders: *Dainik Jagran, Amar Ujala, Dainik Bhaskar, Prabhat Khabar, Rajasthan Patrika* and *Punjab Kesari*. All had staff that could think on their feet and had developed uncanny insights into the way the average Hindi reader's mind worked and how the small-town print market behaved. It was only after Robin Jeffrey (2000: 58) noted that the figures for measuring the combined value of all advertising placed by major agencies and their commission charges were somewhat 'slippery', and in the case of Hindi print media, greatly underestimated, that some unspoken truths began to roll out.

By 2000, apart from major advertising agencies, a whole new, largely unorganised sector that housed small-town advertisers mushroomed. They negotiated directly with marketing staff for the placement of their ads in the edition of the Hindi paper that best serve their interests. It is because of a steady growth in this sector, which caters only to Hindi print, that standalone multi-edition Hindi dailies could survive the attrition after the (post-1995) TV boom. It will be interesting to see, now that the market has trifurcated into print, TV and digital, how each approaches the holy grail of advertising revenue.

Sevanti Ninan (2007: 101) quotes Harivansh Narayan Singh, the then editor of *Prabhat Khabar*, the popular Jharkhand-based Hindi daily, and now a nominated (by Janata Dal [United]) member of India's Rajya Sabha and also its deputy chairman. According to Harivansh, when the mega Hindi dailies, like *Dainik Jagran*, entered Jharkhand, they adroitly utilised various methods developed by his daily to woo the local readership, such as greeting the readers with a '*Johar* Jharkhand!' ('johar' is a tribal term of greeting), launching special editions aimed at the 'intellectual class' and mounting various local interactive programmes. Another mega daily, the Madhya Pradesh-based *Dainik Bhaskar*, did all this and innovated. For example, it announced that it would spend the considerable revenue it earned (around Rs 100,000 a month) from people placing obituary notices in the paper on improving crematoriums in the state. Each daily took care to keep its cover prices affordably low and covered the extra expenses of production with advertising revenues, as the English dailies were already doing. These measures put paid to the early twentieth-century Gandhian model that required that the reader pay the real-time price for the paper, so that editorial freedoms were not compromised at the behest of governmental or corporate advertisers.

HINDI PAPERS GIVE PIGGYBACK RIDES TO ENGLISH INTO SMALL-TOWN INDIA

The end of the twentieth century saw a paradox wherein the metro-based English dailies and their luxury supplements came out with regional editions. These editions then began riding piggyback on Hindi papers. The aim was to mop up whatever readership there was for English to boost their sales figures. Hindi papers that had so far been deprived of quality newsprint and machines had waged their own kind of guerrilla war while wooing the regional markets, without much help from the owners, corporates and the marketing whiz-kids. As they fought for a place in the new markets with their backs to the wall, they had to reinvent themselves and resort to various strategies and innovative techniques for their survival.

Advertising and marketing teams were saddled with pushing pairs of Hindi and English dailies (under the '*jodi*' offer), talk of 'joint branding', of hosting readers' *melas* (rural fairs) and offering cash rewards for jointly pushing for speedy growth. This was a relief, as this, at long last, opened the gates to better technology for Hindi, which was already being used by small town-based dailies like *Nai Dunia* and *Rajasthan Patrika* to great effect. The editorials were told (as though they did not know it) that the ambitious, upwardly-mobile, new Hindi reader wants increasingly to read about trendy lifestyles, the lives of celebrities, and food and eateries, never mind the effect on quality. The newspaper, the suave marketing managers told them, was a product and the Hindi product, with its vast readership, must help the English paper enter non-English reading households.

A devilishly cunning scheme called 'jodi' (two-in-one) was spawned, under which the hugely under-priced English newspapers began to be delivered with the Hindi one, with an introductory offer that slashed prices of both substantially if one subscribed for the jodi. The idea was that English had a certain snob appeal (ground staff called it 'stickiness'), and once the papers were delivered for a year to households that were anyway spending vast amounts of money sending their children to English-medium schools, most of them would continue the subscription. It gave the sagging numbers of English dailies a boost. But while their advertising revenues rose, Hindi papers continued to get downmarket ads for innerwear, bicycles, hair oil and inexpensive footwear.

The New Millennium Formulae

The memory most of us associate with the media of the 2000s is that of unfettered growth, when lists of India's most read dailies and most watched TV programmes began listing only vernacular-based products; and when parliamentarians began waving copies of Hindi dailies in Parliament, demanding action on issues raised by them. The mighty Microsoft worked furiously to attain compatibility with India's vernaculars and Google urged major Hindi dailies to allow it to put their contents online. It all seemed to point to the dawn of a more democratic, more reader-centric era in Indian media. Almost ten years in, enlightenment is hard to find. Most major Hindi dailies are undeniably partisan and happy to use governments' versions of events and root for their schemes wholeheartedly. What happened? How did patterns of political and corporate corruption that our free press exposed and attacked for over half-a-century suddenly become our shared future?

In the Hindi belt, *zar, zoru aur zamin* (gold, women and land), singly or combined, are believed to be the root cause of all frictions. At the end of 2018, print's share of total media revenue declined from 30 per cent to just over 18 per cent. The reason, according to media columnist Vanita Kohli-Khandekar (2019a), is that between 2013 and 2017, media owners, keen to gain maximum revenue from the market, had been fudging and inflating their readership numbers. Each year after the Readership Survey surfaced, heated arguments broke out among bigger publishers about who was the real leader in the market. Meanwhile, both demonetisation and the newly introduced Goods and Services Tax (GST) hit the industry hard. And while the publishers squabbled among themselves, Reliance introduced the much more inexpensive Jio, giving media consumers more choice. Consumption of online news jumped up from 0.8 gigabytes per person per month in 2016 to 8 gigabytes in 2018. This led to a huge uptick in online media (the IRS 2019 recorded over 279 million people reading news online). By 2018, the annual IRS data was almost universally accepted, and acknowledged by media groups and advertisers as the gold standard for judging readership. When the figures for print and digital readership are released, it gives an immediate bump in numbers to both English and vernacular outputs from major media houses. This exercise has especially helped the top 20 online publishers in India, of whom the Times Group, HT Media, India Today Group and the Express Group are on the ball with digital media. Given India's half-open markets fast revising their data and the vernaculars' readership base widening more and more, we will ultimately have informed consumers and the system to beat back fudged numbers and unprofessional marketing practices that have bedevilled the Hindi media.

According to an ABC report (2017), India has managed to buck the global trend of readership decline in print media. A majority of its nearly 500 million smartphone users may be spending longer hours surfing the news on the internet on their mobile screens, but digital news platforms do not seem to have displaced newspapers.

After the 2019 elections, we should not be surprised to see print media readers being subtly assisted by the state when they demand more professional dissemination of news. The print media is seen as infinitely less of a threat to the ruling class compared to the increasingly ratings-driven, 'breaking news'-seeking visual media. And since your enemy's enemy is your friend, the ruling class will not allow market forces to starve the print media at the expense of the visual media.

Since the digital media is growing at a much faster pace, the print media's earlier dominance and ad share is fast being eroded. It is today much more in need of, and dependent on, advertising revenue from government sources. This is why the mainstream print media today appears to be much more supportive of government policies than independent digital news portals. The government, for its part, is spending a great deal of money on print media advertising to promote its social welfare schemes like *Beti Bachao, Beti Padhao* (Save the girl child, educate the girl child). According to the Parliamentary Committee on Empowerment of Women report (2021: 52) tabled in the Lok Sabha during the winter session in December 2021, 78.91 per cent of the total funds released during 2016–19 were spent on media advocacy.

THE BIRTH OF A NEW BOND BETWEEN VERNACULARS AND ENGLISH

Since the beginning of the 2010s, as disposable incomes in small-town India have risen, the great Chinese Wall between English and vernacular publications has begun to crumble. After almost all editors of English dailies, like the Hindi media barons before them, have turned owner-editors, many have quickly sensed the advantage in forming protective guilds across regions. Unbelievable new bands of brothers are now being formed by the marketing managers for formulating new strategies, signing 'no poaching' pacts and sharing information about the best clients and the cleverest (often the most unprofessional) practices. Media barons are no longer dismissive of their vernacular publications, and the Hindi owner-editors are also coming out of their small, simple and static worlds and sending their sons to well-known business schools and putting them through media courses abroad for hands-on training. The vernacular readers may have grown up on a diet of only language papers, but they too are now sending their children to English-medium schools. The new bilingual households of the future are the new focus area, where the action is around India's vernaculars.

By now, it is clear that the media and the socio-economic setting in which it operates are two different things. A certain adversarial relationship between the media, and political parties and corporates was once seen by media practitioners as a basic rule of their turf, and one was expected to verify everything handed to us by sources other than our own. But as the media business has proliferated, this particular cold war has lost its intensity. It would be too deterministic to say that we Indians are programmed to initiate systemic corruption, but there is ample historical evidence to show that secretive understandings to scratch each other's backs between many of our politicians and media owners are not too rare.

The violent revival of age-old caste, communal, and most recently, gender-based divides would surely qualify as the sociological equivalent of a tectonic upheaval in a supposedly modern socialist republic. Today, most major media houses are happily inviting outside capital, owners have become editors and many editors have opted for partnerships. With this, relations between media practitioners and their erstwhile adversaries have begun to assume the character of a great game, enjoyable but non-life threatening. Even the language of reporting reflects it: editorials on coalition politics talk of falling dominoes, theorists frequently build test cricket models of party politics, observers of caste-based coalitions talk almost admiringly of the intricate games of chess being played at state capitals. Implicit in all this, however, is the assumption that the playing field will always remain level, and no matter how intense the mutual suspicion between the press and the ruling parties, neither side will ever think of hurling the chess pieces out of the window and walking away after ripping up the board.

THE ERUPTION OF PAID NEWS

It has taken the seismic jolts and the ugly eruption of paid news to bring the media world to the realisation that we can no longer take the stability of our time-tested journalistic systems for granted. The paid news syndrome has a long subterranean past. It originated along old and deep fault lines that run under our entire media system between the twin tectonic plates of economic globalisation and political fragmentation. The pressures generated by frequent friction between the two have been building for decades and ultimately threaten just about every branch of the media. As the least secure among them, the infrastructure of the vernacular media is simply the first to crack.

Restraining corruption, like unleashing it, requires both capability and resolve. This was hard during the days of one-party rule with a protected mixed economy. In the age of liberalisation, with so many groups competing for the fast-opening Indian market, regional media houses that have, or are about to go public, will face a catch-22. Should they stay small and risk being pushed out by the multi-edition T-Rexes from the Hindi belt? Or should they also mutate and multiply and join the gang? If they survive as regional players, some day they may be in the position to counter the decline in journalistic morals ushered in by the mega media houses, but like the old Soviet Union, even then they will accomplish this only by ceasing to be what they are.

Towards the end of the 1990s, it was amply clear that the health of the Hindi media, as we hurtled towards the new century, needed an urgent balancing of priorities. The prerequisite for this was to develop a perception of the whole, and a greater feel for the actual dynamics of the media industry: the essential relationships between the editorials and the marketing teams, between the editor and the professional CEO, between the lowly rural stringer and the modem operator, between the field and the desk. Deliberations about censorship and the code of ethics for journalists reveal that political behaviour towards the media has been changing. Digital media ensures that there will be a gradual but irreversible trend towards self-governance, away from authority by imposition.

Since the early 1990s, no one denied the need for better ad revenue. However, it should also be conceded that this need was sharpened to a large extent by the artificially lowered cover price of newspapers and the hefty commissions paid to agents, vendors and stringers who were, in many cases, the one and the same as the big publishing houses with deep pockets who tilted the media field in their favour to drive out smaller local players. Since the consumers of the dailies in vernacular were paying more money than the readers of English-language papers and still getting fewer pages, the media establishments should have created and enforced inviolable ad-to-edit ratios, ideally around 70 per cent editorial matter to 30 per cent ads. The key at the top of each ad, the fonts used and the general layout of the page were expected to follow government mandates and reveal to readers that the item was a sponsored ad, not a part of editorial matter. These vital details continued to be overlooked.

The Unreported World of Stringer Reporters

Then there were the stringers. Ever since they were launched, the upcountry editions of most Hindi dailies were short of regular hands to balance budgets. This required clusters of stringers and super-stringers. Most of them signed papers to say that they were not accredited journalists and derived their primary income from other sources. Most received a pittance as an allowance or just an identity card establishing their bona fides as representatives of a particular daily. The reason they still queued up to be appointed as stringers was that they were more than compensated with a regular commission for soliciting local advertising on behalf of the area manager. To mop up all local news, the regional pages were transmitted electronically to the nearest print location at the last minute. They reached the central desk with just minutes to spare before the edition was rushed to the press. This opened the floodgates to unverified and dubious news in editorially policed editions of Hindi dailies. During elections, local or national, the transmitted district pages carried nothing but hagiographies of various candidates from various parties, predicting them as sure-shot winners. In Chapter 4, we shall discuss in some detail why today, more than ever before, the role and recruitment patterns of these stringers merit close scrutiny and clear legal guidelines for all media houses.

As new media outlets grow in the new millennium, the competition for audiences, and even more crucially, for advertising revenue is growing. Since cross-media ownership rules have been slowly dispensed with, commercialised and commodified journalism grows stronger. In a telling phrase, Sanjay Gupta (quoted in Ninan 2007: 106), the editor of the largest Hindi daily, *Dainik Jagran*, with over 70 million readers, terms the addition of local pages to regional editions as 'customisation of localisation'. Certainly a neat idea. But in time, given the unforeseen variables flowing in as the digital age truly began for the Hindi media, it has led to rot seeping into news gathering from metro towns to villages. A reporter in Sultanpur, a small but heavily populated town in Uttar Pradesh, who gathers news for four major Hindi dailies including *Jagran*, confessed to journalist Raksha Kumar (2019) that when he steps out, his explicit intention is not to gather news, but to solicit local ads from the biggest advertisers in Sultanpur—*sari* and toy shops, automobile dealers and cell phone retailers—for the various Hindi papers he represents. The growth of Hindi's major dailies, both in terms of numbers and revenues, may be admirable, but the system it has built to do this has triggered off an unforeseen crisis of credibility in the regional media, particularly in the Hindi belt, that has been electing and sending large numbers to India's Parliament, and most of our prime ministers.

CONCLUSION

As the twentieth century drew to a close, Hindi print had established its numerical superiority over the Indian media. The decadal census of 2001 (RGCCI 2001) revealed that the Hindi states had registered a huge growth in literacy, particularly noticeable in its most backward states—Bihar, Madhya Pradesh, Uttar Pradesh and Rajasthan. The newly energised owners of dailies now began to expand into new territories. This led to spectacular jostling and pushing for numbers, ad revenues and proximity to powerful regional politicians. Initially, the Anglocentric managerial cadres based in metro towns continued to evade the lessons the local managers had learnt over the years and the customised marketing techniques they had used to create loyal readership. But as competition grew among the biggest names—*Dainik Jagran*, *Dainik Bhaskar*, *Hindustan*, *Sahara*, *Prabhat Khabar*—to win over new regions, they learnt to play the game by local rules. Soon, groups like *The Times of India* and *Hindustan Times* also launched their English dailies, benefited by their jodi offers in which the English daily was introduced into Hindi-reading households piggybacking on the popular house Hindi daily. This was also a period when special schemes and multiple gifts and other attractive rewards for readers began to be floated. The senior managers flew in from metro headquarters and inaugurated media interactions in five- or four-star hotel lounges for business. These were replete with attractive PowerPoint presentations detailing the reach and growth of the group.

This focus on the regional editions of dailies resulted in a thaw between Hindi and English in major houses. It led to the best available machinery and computerised workflow systems being deployed for simultaneous printing in both languages. But the downside was that it began corroding and corrupting the public sphere created by the regional media. Most publishing houses employed stringers in large numbers to save costs. These were expected to generate a fixed number of news items, mop up as much local advertising as they could and also keep the local officials 'happy'. The pay was low, but the percentile bonuses made their jobs worthwhile, in addition to lending them a chance to interact with local officials, with whom they often developed a 'you-scratch-my-back-I-scratch-yours' camaraderie.

The Hindi media gave increased importance to political power, which began to be utilised by many owners to accrue various benefits for their other businesses. Occasionally, guided by their political mentors, some publishers began to fine-tune the selection and promotion of embedded journalists. The earlier breed of editors at this point became somewhat redundant as editors began to be recruited on the basis of their proximity to the political party in power, and their ability to solicit favours for the owners. Several owners and a few editors were nominated to the Upper House of Parliament by political supremos, a few were nominated as ambassadors or as directors to the boards of public-sector banks or various bodies associated with the Rajbhasha Vibhag, which monitored the use of Hindi in various public-sector enterprises.

Thus, Hindi media stepped into the twenty-first century, a volatile media-driven age of mass politics, populist leaders who spoke in nothing but vernaculars, and Hindi being fast-forwarded by India's right-wing parties as a symbol of pan-Indian nationalism. Their potent efforts to homogenise Hindi and Hindu culture created moral biases and deepened Hindi's hold over the national discourse at the same time. This was a Hindi media, many of us realised with dismay, that was in danger of becoming, like the class that created and promoted it, a middle-class culture full of political smugness and a dangerously isolationist view of nationalism.

4

Living above Fault-Lines

Looking back at the first decade of the twenty-first century, it seems like an age of unfettered growth for vernacular print media, particularly Hindi. Hindi publications dominated the lists of India's top 10 most read dailies and other periodicals. And ratings for Hindi programming (both news and entertainment) on TV soared above similar programmes in English. During parliamentary debates, many parliamentarians waved their copies of popular Hindi dailies and demanded explanations for queries raised or scandals reported. The mighty Microsoft realised the worth of India's vernaculars and intense work was done to make their hardware more compatible with the needs of Hindi users. Google also began contacting major Hindi dailies, offering them space to put their content online. This led many to believe that India was looking at the dawn of a new era, far more democratic and vernacular reader-centric than ever before. Ten years later, it became hard to substantiate that fleeting vision. Today, most major Hindi dailies are clearly partisan and seem willing to buy the government's version of events and root for various new schemes wholeheartedly. The journalists covering the government realised that the government had been politely but firmly denying them access to cabinet notes and limiting ministerial exchanges.

WHAT HAPPENED?

How did patterns of political and corporate opacity and censorship, which our free press had periodically managed to penetrate and castigate through their writings for over half-a-century, suddenly become the media's future? In hindsight, it is clear that the trend started way back when liberalisation, deregulation and privatisation of the media industry had led to the unprecedented growth of the Hindi media and its revenues. In the new millennium, there was also an increase in international investment in media structures and digital platforms. This led to the speeding up of digital delivery and installation of new distribution systems. The traditional newspaper clipping business underwent a paradigm shift. Sophisticated software arrived that could trawl through millions of websites and pick up and tag news articles for their clients in the media efficiently and accurately within seconds. All this opened up new platforms and markets for both Hindi print media and all its digital communication platforms. At this point, no one was willing to wait and take note of the basic fact that despite its extraordinary expansion, the digitised and globalised Hindi media remained oligopolistic and had not effectively improved its fragile and semi-skilled editorial structures as required. Also, the socio-politically volatile area that the media infrastructure stood on hid within it several ancient caste, class and communal fault-lines that the political class could throw into motion to carve out vote-banks. The absence of restrictions on cross-media ownership strengthened monopolies, both vertically (across various kinds of media) and horizontally (control over regional distribution systems for various media products). As a result, the new digital connectivity in the first two decades of the twenty-first century mostly resulted in the proliferation of infotainment-driven and sensationalist content for Hindi media. As the precious public sphere created by the Hindi media in the last century slipped into the hands of a growing consolidation of big media companies, the needs of the shareholders, not the humble readers, took precedence. Debates began to be manipulated to the advantage of the corporate and political bosses, and coverage of issues like rural or urban poverty, environmental degradation, and real developmental issues in general began to shrink.

THE 2014 ELECTION AS A GAME CHANGER

In such a scenario, an election is where the varying economic interests of rural and urban India, and the ruling political party and its opponents collide. This resulted, in 2014, in a series of sudden quakes releasing dangerous levels of subterranean heat and energy. The commercial advertisers, on whose ratings the edifice of media had come to rest, and the political party, with its capacity for producing vast advertising revenues, swung into action. Since 2014, old media hands have seen an undeniable growth in numbers of embedded journalists in most media organisations. Ironically, the new government aggressively promoted Hindi as India's only potential *rashtra bhasha* (national language), but with its already flawed inner structure, docile editorials and political linkages, Hindi media became even more wary of exercising editorial autonomy. The recent freezing of vital government advertising for three English dailies (see Reuters 2019), with a combined readership of over 26 million, allegedly as retaliation for their critical stances on several major decisions of the government, further underscored to the multi-media Hindi publishers that it was best to support the government in all matters and be happy with the unsurprisingly large growth in their numbers and annual revenues. Most major Hindi dailies meekly accepted the official versions of events handed to them by government functionaries, to the near exclusion of all other viewpoints.

This chapter is an effort to explore some of the active fault-lines that lie beneath the Hindi media's public sphere and understand how they relate to its rise in numbers and the simultaneous loss of its hard-earned aura of independence.

HINDI'S MULTI-MEDIA OWNER-EDITORS AND MANAGERIAL CLASS

India has long debated the issue of media monopolies and cross-media ownership. During the early years after Independence, the 'jute press' was criticised often by political leaders. This was a clear reference to big media groups like the Hindustan Times Group and the Times Group, both of whose owners were businessmen and jute barons. Similarly, the ownership of steel plants by a few influential media barons led occasionally to derisive references to the dominance of the 'steel press'. Soon, pressure built up to frame laws preventing large media monopolies.

With 22 recognised Indian languages and fast proliferating segments in print, digital media, radio and television, the mediascape in India has presented a complex scenario. By the 1970s, most major media entities had come to be variously owned and controlled either by individuals or by various trusts, societies and corporate bodies. According to the findings of the Media Ownership Monitor (MOM) report, four major dailies in Hindi—*Dainik Jagran*, *Hindustan Dainik*, *Amar Ujala* and *Dainik Bhaskar*—today control 76.45 per cent of the total readership for Hindi papers nationally (Reporters without Borders and DataLEADS 2019a). All four are owned in large part by the families of the original founders. All have, by now, acquired an impressive array of other media platforms in the digital world. This provides them with a clear advantage over other vernaculars and enormous economic clout and political leverage in the 11 states of the Hindi belt. By the first decade of the new millennium, large TV and broadcast networks began acquiring/partnering with regional players. Then came the realisation that in the years to come, the scope for multi-media expansion is going to be far bigger in Indian languages, particularly in Hindi.

The TRAI and Questions about Cross-Media Ownership

Fearing the loss of healthy heterogeneity and fair competition in the media market, in February 2009, the Telecom Regulatory Authority of India (TRAI) advised the government that necessary safeguards were needed to ensure plurality and diversity in print, radio and television. This advice was vociferously questioned by media owners in the publications and TV channels they owned. It was said that if restrictions were imposed on cross-media ownership, the multiplicity and growth of the media would be badly impacted. The pro-cross-media ownership lobby also said the market in India was too diverse to allow media monopolies to come up. A little later, in July 2009, another 200-page report was submitted by the Administrative Staff College of India (ASCI) to the Ministry of Information and Broadcasting. This report recommended the strict implementation of laws preventing cross-media ownership to ward off market dominance by a few corporates with diverse interests in sectors like steel, aviation, hotels, cement, education, textiles, cricket and automobiles (Guha Thakurta 2012a).

The implementation of the report was hotly resisted by big players in the field. Their boards gradually all but eliminated journalists and brought in investment bankers, venture capitalists, chartered accountants, corporate lawyers, retailers and representatives of major companies who were also big advertisers. This, as the TRAI feared, led to many questionable dealings and a confusion of priorities in all branches of the media.

According to a comprehensive report on such unfair practices by senior journalist Paranjoy Guha Thakurta (2012b), our weak to non-existent laws on cross-media ownership had led to a scenario where a few mega-companies and corporations dominated the market, and media pluralism as we had known it was fast evaporating. Aided by global trends, ownership of print, radio, TV and websites across various regions and languages had also begun feeding and fattening these oligopolies that protected, supported and networked closely with each other, and went on to be represented in the most important media bodies.

At such a juncture, to bring in transparency, Reporters without Borders and DataLEADS launched Media Ownership Monitor—an extensive, openly available database that tracks the ownership of media houses in India. Using the 2018 data from the Registrar of Newspapers in India, they show that India is one of the biggest media markets in the world. In 2018, India had 118,239 registered publications (38,000 weekly newspapers, 36,564 monthly magazines and 17,160 dailies). It also had 880 satellite channels, 550 FM and community radio stations and over 380 news channels. The only news radio station, All India Radio, remained a government monopoly. By January 2019, they had evaluated 58 media outlets—25 print, 23 TV outlets, 9 websites and 1 radio station. The ownership of all these rested in 39 companies and 45 individual owners (Reporters without Borders and DataLEADS 2019c). One of the key findings of the report is:

Within the sample of this study, as many as ten media owners have direct or indirect links with politics while some of them even represent a political party. There are countless others however, who have refused to declare their political affiliations, but yet own media companies. Between them, media owners with political links control a sizeable share of viewership/readership. (Reporters without Borders and DataLEADS 2019b)

So far, actual interaction with the managerial teams has shown that publishing houses continue to mediate with the small-town markets through a lower-ranking posse of managers in charge of their Hindi publications. They are quick to quote reports prepared by foreign ratings agencies, to whom the Hindi belt is the single largest homogenised market in the country, but many variables (such as the pulls and pressures and the cultural, linguistic and ethnic diversity of these 11 populous states, from the central states to the Himalayan states of Himachal Pradesh and Uttarakhand, and to Bihar and Jharkhand in the east) are largely absent from their media planning.

Paid Insertions: News that Dare Not Speak its Name

It would be churlish to blame the government of the day for putting the squeeze on the media. The truth about Indian media's increasing reliance on revenues generated by news that has been paid for has been debated since the late Prabhash Joshi raised it. He was followed by an explosive report on the phenomenon of paid news by Guha Thakurta (2012b). But the subject remained shrouded in half-truths, corporate denials and misleading information. In 2013, when the Anna Andolan was at its peak, the city supplement of one of the biggest multi-edition Hindi dailies in India carried a whole page of classified advertising that extended support for the fasting Anna Hazare and his men. Smiling engagingly in ads, leaders from small-town and rural India could be seen in the classified section, extending their heartfelt support to Hazare's cause, nestling cosily next to ads for reducing fat, increasing male potency and height. Almost all the ads carried the mugshots and phone numbers of those who had paid for the insertions (one was even wearing a '*Main Anna hoon*' [I am Anna] T-shirt). Close examination revealed the advertisers to be local builders, heads of charitable religious trusts, educational bodies, regional organisations for migrant workers from

Bihar, social workers heading various *sanghs* (guilds) and *sangathans* (organisations) to save India ('*Bharat bachao*'), and various resident welfare associations. This was the beginning of the re-feudalisation of Hindi media.

THE DARK UNDERBELLY OF READERSHIP DATA

In 2019, India emerged as the largest publisher in the world with close to 6,700 publications and over 260 million copies distributed daily. According to the latest certified language-wise figures released by the ABC for the period January–November 2018, Hindi publications continue to top the charts. Among the top three Indian dailies, two are in Hindi: *Dainik Bhaskar* and *Dainik Jagran*. Both showed growth from 2017 figures. The English daily, *The Times of India* (Mumbai), is at the third spot.

Money, general elections and monopolies proved to be an interesting combination for the Hindi media by the end of the twentieth century. But ironically, with this humongous growth reversing global trends, the Hindi media, it seems, has entered a sort of Habermasian third phase: that of 're-feudalisation'. During this phase, Habermas predicted, the state and corporates will seize control of the lucrative media businesses and the public sphere will degenerate till the media becomes a mass 'product' and the reader a mindless consumer driven by advertisers' choices, not his own (see Jeffrey 2000: 11–13). While this is not a very pleasant thought, it is fast becoming a reality. The incumbent Indian government reportedly spent millions on Hindi print advertising and, in January 2019, has even raised the rates for the coveted DAVP ads by 25 per cent (Jha and Tewari 2019). This is the vital monetary input that allows Hindi media barons to sell their newspapers for about one-sixth of their production costs. Cash-rich political parties and candidates have all increasingly capitalised on their power to disburse favours, like the allocation of cheap land for factories and releasing DAVP ads to friendly media owners. The politically volatile Hindi belt, with many powerful media barons and editors sitting in the Upper House as nominees of the ruling party, has benefited the most from such largesse.

The movers and shakers now seem far more sensitive to reporting in the digital and visual media than the more compliant print. A subtle effort therefore seems to be afoot to strengthen the print media through advertising. The source of news for the average Hindi reader by the first decade of the twenty-first century began shifting from good old print to digital. With over 600 million Facebook users and 400 million monthly active users of (Facebook-owned) WhatsApp in India, Hindi publishers are coming to realise that print is about to lose its lead in the field to digital (Thussu 2016: viii). The other problem is that the Hindi media's expanding footprint is accompanied by a large trust deficit between the papers and their readers, who realise that the government and its leadership holds the mainstream media in contempt. As Sevanti Ninan (2019) points out in an article, between 2014 and 2019, constant tirades against the media have been unleashed, often by senior members of the ruling party and its official representatives on multiple media platforms. The ruling party simply changed the rules of engagement with the media. Starved of direct interaction with the movers and shakers, major media houses began sponsoring annual events and inviting the prime minister and major ministers to generate exclusive news. But for the public, the notion of a fearless media and a government that seeks it out to reach the public stand deeply scarred today.

Most editors and celebrity anchors are seen neither as the gatekeepers nor the last court of appeal for news that they put out in the public sphere. On all contentious subjects, from demonetisation to the Balakot 'surgical strike', the official media has been able to seize the moment, and with this, it is the government that controls the narrative. Social media websites like Twitter and Facebook are full of messages from media followers saying that during elections and the events following the abrogation of Article 370, the Hindi media has been largely putting out the official versions handed to them by the government's media cell, verbatim.

Censorship, Self-Censorship and a Gradual Delegitimisation

Between 2014 and 2019, as media creation and media use grew explosively, the government and its agencies began strategising on how to use the multiple media platforms now available to millions in India. Inexpensive internet connectivity and the steady expansion of social media between 2016 and 2018 led to a 65 per cent growth in media, whose users numbered 500 million (Narayanan and Pradhan 2016). Then Facebook (with 294 million Indian accounts already in existence) acquired popular messaging service WhatsApp in 2014, adding 200 million more users. When Reliance launched its 4G telecom services, the resultant tariff war deepened internet penetration even more.

Between 2014 and 2019, the Indian media began to experience a new kind of media management. In 2014, the World Hindi Conference was launched with great fanfare in Bhopal, the capital of Hindi-speaking Madhya Pradesh. The organisers took care not to invite eminent Hindi intellectuals, several of whom had been recipients of major awards, on the grounds that they had, in the past, proved to be rather aggressive contrarians. At a session on Hindi media, students from the local college of journalism were similarly dissuaded from attending. The stated reason was that the session was to apprise party workers of how the Hindi media functions on the ground. One of the chief organisers of the Hindi festival of letters was a retired general who was then a minister of state. He told the media that most journalists and writers were likely to misbehave, and used the pejorative 'presstitute' for the combative representatives of the media. Since then, every minister for information and broadcasting and the prime minister himself have repeatedly questioned the adversarial media's credibility.

Within that kind of atmosphere, a slow but dangerous delegitimisation of the mainstream media is emerging. The Prime Minister's Office (PMO) no longer holds the usual pressers and a stop has been put to the age-old practice of allowing a posse of journalists on the prime ministerial plane, so that while he is travelling abroad, he can informally, and if he wishes, individually, talk with senior media representatives. The members of the Central cabinet too maintain a studied distance from the mainstream media. The prime minister prefers to bypass the media and speak directly to the public in rallies and through weekly addresses in his *Mann Ki Baat* broadcast on the state-owned All India Radio.

The years 2014–20 have also witnessed a steady rise in trolling of media men, and in particular, women, who are critical of the way things are run, or raise uncomfortable questions regarding public policies. Meanwhile, physical violence is rising. In 2017, Gauri Lankesh, the Bengaluru-based editor of the Kannada weekly, *Lankesh Patrike*, founded by her father, who had been a steady critic of the right-wing's unleashing of violence against their opponents in the state, was shot dead (Gettleman and Kumar 2017). Another freelance Hindi journalist, critical of the Chhattisgarh government's oppression of tribals, was first jailed as a Naxal sympathiser and then barred from the state (*Scroll.in* 2017). And a senior editor in the Northeast barely escaped being killed by a petrol bomb hurled at her office (Saikia 2018).

While some vernacular media hands asserted their right to freedom of expression, many mainstream media outlets began to justify the concept of self-censorship publicly. Several Hindi news dailies and channels dropped news and stories deemed hostile to or critical of the government. Corporate India also created pressure on media teams to exercise restraint in reporting corporate crimes. When a powerful media owner couple was involved in a murder case involving a member of their own family, the media were careful not to name any of their several erstwhile corporate connections, and several senior media men and women even wrote against the brutal treatment the media was giving them by reporting their sordid family details to the public. Several major scams involving banks, power and mining companies, and real-estate barons were similarly underplayed.

The Criminal Justice System and the Media

According to Reporters without Borders (2002, 2019), in the field of freedom for the press, India, which stood at the 80th rank out of 139 countries in 2002, stood in 2019 at 140 out of 180 countries, even lower than violence-prone nations like Sudan and Afghanistan. This rank fell further to 142 in the 2020 World Press Freedom Index, and in 2022, India's rank had fallen even further, showing a steep decline to 150 out of 180 countries (Sampath 2022). What is especially worrisome is that across party lines, all post-Independence governments have tended to use a highly questionable colonial-era law against sedition to suppress freedom of expression by bringing in motivated cases against the free media in lower courts, aimed mainly to intimidate and harass investigative journalists. As the historian Ramachandra Guha, a biographer of Gandhi, reminds us, after being released from jail, Gandhi had called for the peoples of India to rise against the law, which, in his words, 'was established by the naked sword, kept ready to descend on us at will of the arbitrary rulers' (quoted in Guha 2019). The same Section 124A of the Indian Penal Code that the British had used against Gandhi in 1922 (for his writings critical of the colonial government in his paper, *Young India*) was used almost a century later in 2019 to file a criminal case in Bihar against a group of some 50 highly respected artists and intellectuals. The charge is that a letter they wrote in July 2019 was violative of Sections 124A (sedition), 153B (assertion prejudicial to national integration), 290 (public nuisance), 297 (trespass to wound religious feelings), and last but not least, 504 (intentional insult) (ibid.). Cases of defamation were earlier filed as civil cases, but now the trend is to file them under the criminal category, which is infinitely more serious and involves prolonged and expensive litigation.

GENDER AND WOMEN IN THE HINDI MEDIA

'At the end of the 20th century women in journalism in India are either inching forward or striding forward depending on whether one is describing the many or the few,' writes senior journalist Sevanti Ninan (2000: ix), in her Foreword to Ammu Joseph's *Women in Journalism: Making News*. In her concluding chapter, Joseph (2000: 291, 302–03) underscores this further,

> [W]omen in journalism ... cannot be clubbed into a single stereotypical category.... Women journalists are crucial to this process of feminising the press.... [M]edia products are constantly shaped and re-shaped by the human beings who produce them. Their knowledge and ideas, their powers of observation and analysis, their beliefs and assumptions, their opinions and prejudices determine the nature and content of the media and its messages.

In July 2019, an interesting report, *Gender Inequalities in Indian Media* (a joint initiative of UN Women and Media Rumble), based on a six-month study of six English and seven Hindi dailies up to March 2019, was released. The report, quoted at length by Geetika

Mantri (2019), notes that there is a pronounced gender gap visible within the media cadres and in the amount of coverage news items about women received. Compared to men, very few leadership roles (editor-in-chief, managing editor, executive editor, bureau chief, input/output editors) were assigned to women. In print, the percentage of women in these positions was 13.6 per cent of the total, and in TV news channels, it was 20.9 per cent. Digital portals had the highest number of women leaders, at 26.3 per cent.

Of the 6,806 articles surveyed in Hindi, only 11 per cent were authored by women. Among four major Hindi dailies, on top of the pile were *Amar Ujala* (20 per cent); *Hindustan* (7 per cent), and *Rajasthan Patrika* and *Punjab Kesari* (5 per cent each). Women journalists, the report notes, were assigned writing mostly on 'soft' subjects like culture and women's issues. Women correspondents were glaringly absent from traditional 'hard' beats like politics, national security, defence and sports.

All the dailies, to their credit, carried stories related to women and gender issues on their front pages, but only 3 per cent of these front-page news items were about women, 50 per cent of which had been filed by women. Among popular Hindi magazines, *Sarita* (published by the Delhi Press Group) claims to be a magazine for women, promoting radical ideas. But 84.7 per cent of articles published in it were authored by males.

TV news did slightly better vis-à-vis women's visibility because it was felt that the viewers liked to see young and pretty faces as anchors. However, when panel discussions were analysed, there seemed to be a preponderance of males, even in panels discussing major reports of rapes, women farmers and marginal workers. In 75 per cent of panels surveyed on two Hindi channels, NDTV India and India TV, men from various disciplines and backgrounds comprised 75 per cent of panels, whereas the women representing their gender were mostly senior bureaucrats, defence and financial experts or representatives of eminent think tanks.

Digital news media presented a slightly more female-friendly profile. More women covered 'hard' news here. In *The Print*, for example, women made up 72.3 per cent of the total. Some English-language websites had newsrooms with as many as 50 per cent female employees. But among popular digital news portals in Hindi, the picture looked different. The newsrooms of *Newslaundry* (Hindi), *Swarajya* and *Satyagraha* had 88.6, 79.7 per cent and 78.1 per cent males, respectively. Of the 21,000 articles surveyed, only 3.7 per cent dealt directly with gender issues.

DALIT WRITERS AND THE HINDI MEDIA

At a 2016 conference of the Network of Women in Media, India (NWMI), an informal collective of women journalists, the Dalit woman journalist, Jeya Rani (2016), raised a sharp question. Suppose, she said, just suppose that tomorrow a law is enacted that makes it mandatory for the media to prioritise and publish/telecast news of every atrocity against Dalits each day, failing which they will lose their license, what will happen? They will be overwhelmed. Because every minute, a Dalit somewhere is raped, tortured or subjected to abuse. 'The mainstream media is not for the poor, not for the oppressed.... Most certainly not for the Dalits,' she said. Harsh words, but true in the light of known facts.

Quoting a study by the non-governmental organisation (NGO) Oxfam India and *Newslaundry*, a major media watch website, Nithya Subramanian (2019) reports that out of 121 management posts in top Indian print media houses, 106 were occupied by people from the upper castes and the rest by those from the Other Backward Classes (OBCs). There were no Dalits. On Hindi TV news channels, among 40 anchors, three out of four were upper caste. And 70 per cent of panellists participating in prime-time discussions also belonged to the upper castes.

In his 2013 study on Dalit voices in the media, commissioned by *The Hoot*, a website on the media (launched by the NGO, the Media Foundation), senior Delhi-based journalist Ajaz Ashraf (2013) corroborates the dominance of upper castes in India's newsrooms. Of the 21 working Dalit journalists he contacted, 19 confessed to having been subjected to caste-based slurs or asides. The number of Dalit journalists in the mainstream media has risen in the last two decades, but they are nowhere proportionate to their total percentage (15 per cent) of India's population.

Another interesting fact is that the Dalits in the Hindi belt do not subscribe to the notion that schooling their children in government-run Hindi-medium schools will help them rise in life. Early in the first decade of his popular Hindi blog, Ravish Kumar (see Pande 2009a) reported that the Dalit writer and thinker, Chandra Bhan Prasad, had declared English to be the great opener of locks for India's Dalits. Prasad had declared that the birthday of English *Devi* (goddess) will henceforth be celebrated on Lord Thomas Macaulay's birthday. The role of the man and the global language he first introduced into the Indian school system are worthy of veneration, he said.

The Brave New World of Technology as a Disruptor

Speaking at the annual convocation of the Asian College of Journalism in Chennai in 2019, Bloomberg News's editor-in-chief, John Micklethwait (2019), supported Prasad's worldview. He pointed out how, from Gutenberg's press to Tim Berners-Lee's World Wide Web, with innovations such as the telegram, the radio and the television in between, technology has carefully reshaped and changed journalism. And not always for the worse. Having learnt to handle computers and the internet, at the end of the 2010s, Hindi journalism is grappling once again with the twin concepts of artificial intelligence and machine learning hovering above their heads.

So far, information about them and the terminologies used have been available only in English. But it is obvious that in the decades to come, machines will deeply affect and alter the functioning of today's newsrooms and traditional staff hierarchies in several ways. The thing to see is how much responsibility the partner platforms will take for the news they feed us with. How transparent are they? How do their algorithms work? What they permit on their platforms can also be abused. And when that happens, as it did during the 2019 elections (Dasgupta and Guha Thakurta 2019; PTI 2019a), there are few protections in the digital advertising ecology to bar bad actors. Faith that the internet is inherently virtuous, and that choice and universal access always lead to good are theories yet to be tested fully in our democracy.

For the time being, we would be better served by some sort of tectonic thinking. Since the simultaneous pursuit of both democracy and larger market share results in straddling a fault-line, it would be foolish not to prepare for frequent seismic jolts of varying intensity. For this, we will need to go back to the legal system and demand a redefinition of the ownership of news in the print line. In all media outfits today, ad rate cards are being created, agencies are being solicited, and various kinds of group advertising are being handled entirely by their marketing managers. Under such circumstances, how can the editor alone be held responsible for the questionable ads appearing in the paper?

Ads, as we all know by now, are now sent to the printing presses through a SAP dummy (Systems Applications, Products in Data Processing; the SAP dummy material is used to create a sales document item with a bill of service) without so much as a 'by-your-leave' to the editorial. At the time of assembling the day's paper, all the editorial knows on any given day is how much space is marked for ads on each page. To complicate matters further, multi-edition vernacular dailies must have different local and national ad ratios for each upcountry edition, which the area unit manager organises through the seasons. His promotions and annual bonuses depend on the volumes he delivers, never mind if he bullies the stringers and local correspondents into soliciting ads through their local 'connections'. Given this situation, it is time the media reinforced the bleachers by demanding that the ad manager's and/or the area unit manager's name also be included with the resident editor's and the publisher's in the print line for each of the regional editions.

The need for ad revenue is sharpened by the artificially low cost of newspapers and high commissions paid to vendors. Big publishing houses with deep pockets thus have an advantage in the market, and often set the prices of Hindi papers higher than their English counterparts. Clear guidelines on ad-to-edit ratios and marking of sponsored articles will serve to lessen the disparity.

THE INVISIBLE STRINGERS IN THE NEW MILLENNIUM

Upcountry editions of most Hindi dailies are run by a cluster of stringers and super-stringers. They are not accredited journalists and most receive a pittance as an allowance or just an identity card establishing their bona fides as representatives of a particular daily. Their remuneration as news gatherers is mostly laughable. Some of the largest Hindi newspapers pay those manning their modem centres less than the daily wage of a worker under the Mahatma Gandhi National Rural Employment Guarantee Act (MGNREGA), 2005. But the percentile bonuses from ad gathering remain attractive. With such bounty available, along with the clout a media identity card gets you in small-town India, many young men and women are keen to be picked up as unaccredited stringers.

Gathering news fast became an overriding concern for regional news gatherers in the Hindi belt. Given that they had to get the page ready and electronically delivered to be added to the main edition so it could be checked and sent to press on time, they worked on tight deadlines, especially during major events like elections or natural calamities. As for legal or financial protection against work-related mishaps, stringers do not have any. In August 2019, a UP-based stringer, working for one of the largest circulating Hindi dailies, was shot in broad daylight (Rai 2019). While it was front-page news for most dailies, English as also Hindi, the newspaper that was his primary employer did not carry news of the sensational murder on the first day. The role, recruitment and retainership patterns of stringers, therefore, also merit close scrutiny and clear legal guidelines for all media houses.

Conclusion

The Hindi media entered the new century riding on the fresh waves of liberalisation, deregulation, privatisation and international investment in media, both old and new. It began a period of consolidation and mergers of major publishing houses who soon became multi-media. The ownership patterns, however, remained oligopolistic. Most major publishers handed businesses to their own offspring, many of whom had been sent to eminent business schools in the USA and had come back brimming with new ideas for the expansion and reshaping of boardrooms. The old-style managers made way for suave business school-trained managers, for most of whom the Hindi product did not matter much, but the market it opened up did. They introduced Hindi editorials to new technology and launched e-papers for their successful house print dailies. The editors gradually lost their aura and authority. They began reporting more and more to the managers, who themselves took their orders from the boardrooms that now contained venture capitalists, oil, cement or steel barons, auto producers, textile magnates and bankers.

The re-feudalisation of ownership patterns and the new cadre of managers together introduced the phenomenon of 'paid news'. Major newspapers signed deals with various companies, ensuring a greater prominence for issues they wished to see displayed. From this to total compliance to the system was but a short step. With 600 million Facebook users and 400 million active monthly users of WhatsApp, India fast became the new destination for global media giants. As the mainstream media became more and more compliant, the editors began to be seen mostly as sales managers, and a steady stream of invectives against the critical media let loose by the ruling party at the Centre belittled the image of the media in the eyes of the public—the mainstream media became cash-rich, but lost its mojo. Censorship and self-censorship became more common than ever before and several investigative journalists who dared to stand up to mafia groups or corrupt policemen were killed in 'encounters' or hauled up under criminal defamation charges.

The period saw an increase in the number of women journalists, but the Hindi media still remained largely a male turf. There was a slight increase in serious analysis and coverage of issues related to women in the poverty sector and the rise in crimes against women, but coverage of larger issues related to the unorganised sector or farming from the viewpoint of women workers remained elusive. Almost the same treatment was revealed vis-à-vis the Dalits. They are even more poorly represented in the Hindi media than women. But given the rise of several aggressive and vocal activist writers in the community, issues regarding their lives and livelihoods are now treated with more circumspection.

What Hindi media needs now is a balancing of its editorial priorities. It needs legal reforms to provide greater relief and professional freedoms, especially for field reporters, who regularly face physical threats and attacks. Along with this, the laws regarding managerial accountability and cross-media ownership need to be tweaked carefully and applied forcefully to dissuade the big fish from becoming bigger and the voice of regional media from being silenced by regional editions of mega dailies and their digital portals.

5

Who Moved My News? Digitised Media and Expansionism

Between 2014 and 2019, the Indian media industry underwent a tremendous expansion. The number of registered newspapers stood at around 100,000. In addition to this, there were also nearly 400 news channels, with 150 new ones awaiting clearance by the government. The Indian Readership Survey 2017 (with a sample size of 320,000) recorded a 45 per cent growth in Hindi print since 2014. This roughly translates into 176 million readers. The 2014 survey had pegged readership at 121 million (MRUC 2017).

Internet use has also been growing steadily in Hindi. A study jointly conducted by KPMG and Google (2017) recorded that between 2011 and 2016, the internet user base in Hindi grew by 41 per cent. The study predicted that by 2021, vernacular language users, further spurred and aided by internet-enabled devices and services (smartphones, availability of high-speed internet, digital news and social media platforms) will account for 75 per cent of the total internet users in India. Of these, Hindi-language internet users will account for 38 per cent of the total user base. The April 2019 release from the Media Research Users Council (MRUC) and Nielsen puts the numbers of Hindi print media consumers at 425 million, up from the earlier 407 million. In the words of Sanjay Gupta, CEO of the highest selling Indian Hindi daily *Dainik Jagran*, these numbers have 'once again reiterated the power of print' (quoted in Amin 2018).

Apart from the very successful Jagran group, the rest of the Hindi media experienced regular deals and mergers, all of which went on to create complex, multi-layered financial agreements and sales. All this has deeply impacted and changed the Hindi media landscape. According to the May 2019 report from the Media Ownership Monitor, prepared by Reporters without Borders and DataLEADS (2019a), cross-media ownership has grown steadily. The Times Group (that publishes *The Times of India* in English and *Navbharat Times* in Hindi) also owns 14 news channels, one music channel and four movie channels. In addition, it owns 15 newspapers, one online umbrella entity (*India Times*), one FM radio channel, and five internet properties.

The TV Today group (which publishes the best-selling news weekly, *India Today*, both in English and Hindi) likewise also owns four media channels, of which two are in Hindi. The Zee Group, one of the earliest birds in the Hindi TV news scene, owns 14 news channels, one English newspaper, one website and 15 digital properties.

A Brief History of Hindi's Digitisation

In 1995, India's VSNL formally inaugurated the internet for use in India, and in 2020, the internet will complete a quarter century of its availability to the Indian public. The internet was initially introduced in 1986 as a tool for educational and research use. Two years later, the National Informatics Centre (NIC) launched NICNET (NIC Network) to improve intra-ministerial functioning in the Government of India. Education and Research Network (ERNET), a collaborative venture between the Department of Electronics and the United Nations Development Programme (UNDP), which funded it, was also launched. Things changed rapidly once the Broadband Policy was introduced by the government, and after the 3G spectrum was auctioned, many major players entered the market.

Since 2014, the government has promised a major push for vernacular-friendly digitisation. But for an appreciable increase in interactivity, it needs to invest first in the basics, such as improved and vernacular-friendly keyboards for the inexpensive laptops and smartphones it distributes freely. The next-gen ticketing system of the Indian Railways, IRCTC, for example, is one of the world's greatest e-commerce companies, but for small-town and rural customers, it remains very difficult to get bookings done through this facility using

Hindi or any vernacular. The rural *grameen* banking systems similarly remain hard to access for Hindi users.

GLOBAL GIANTS LEAD INNOVATION FOR A USER-FRIENDLY INTERNET FOR VERNACULARS

It is indeed ironic that like the staff at Fort William College in the early nineteenth century, it is not Indian but foreign companies that first saw the vast untapped potential of Hindi for creating a public sphere and openings in the market through social media. They are now creating the needed fonts and technology to formalise and draw users of digitised Hindi towards the internet.

The government has shown a keenness to push for e-commerce. But it is Google and Facebook that have so far done a better job on the ground. Since English covers only 11 per cent of the total users of the internet in India, they are busy exploring and improving their audio typing facilities. And if they succeed, that would cross the proverbial last mile barrier for Indian vernaculars, including Hindi, and bring them into the digital world.

The World Bank has defined the new information technology (IT) in three broad terms: hardware, software, networks (see Pandey 2016: 221). The Hindi media's task is to learn, as fast as possible, how to handle the various goods, applications and services that face it.

Creation of Fonts for the New Media

A deep disparity in the creation of fonts for English and for Indian languages has been a constant feature of the publishing scene in India since its earliest days. In 1834, when the Nirnaya Sagar Press first began to publish Sanskrit texts, they had to establish their own type foundry and use hand lettering for both their Gujarati and Hindi texts. A real decolonisation of script in the graphics and design industry has come 150 years later, in the twenty-first century.

IT companies began to focus and invest in localisation only in the first two decades of the century. Initial breakthroughs came with specially commissioned tasks awarded to some eminent institutes (the Indian Institutes of Technology [IITs]) in India. The initial results required compatible platforms at the receiving end. For example, in

2001, Microsoft Windows first introduced its much-used Mangal font for the Nagari script. It was designed specifically for their system by an academic type designer and professor of calligraphy at IIT Bombay, R. K. Joshi. By 2004, customised Hindi fonts were developed by Tiro Typeworks of Britain, for Vodafone. Fedra, another Hindi typeface, was launched in 2009. The first open-source font for Indian scripts, Mukta, was developed in 2014. It supported Hindi (Dev Nagari script), and also Gujarati, Gurumukhi, Bengali and Tamil. The majority of font designers preferred to work for major companies that provided them with large, commissioned projects.

The Holy Grail: A Unicode Standard for Hindi

Two centuries after the need for a standardised Hindi threw unimaginable new challenges before the Bhakha munshis of Fort William College (in 1805), the globalised economy of the twenty-first century and the vast Hindi markets it opened posed a similar challenge before the tech giants of the West: Google, Facebook and Amazon. The untapped socio-economic and political potential of the vast Hindi market urgently underscored the need for inventing a high quality, multi-script Indic font. Ultimately, the Unicode Consortium, of which India is a member, came up with the now popular Unicode Standard. Unicode is a copyrighted standardisation to which Unicode fonts are built. It defines three blocks for the Dev Nagari script that can also be used for Indic scripts other than Hindi, Marathi, Nepali, Sindhi and Sanskrit, among others. A Unicode Standard character code for Indic languages with Brahmi script is designed to be a multilingual encoding system that requires no switching between scripts. Today, various tech companies purchase Unicode to design their own fonts or for their front vendors. Many vendors today offer their products for free downloading.

Before Unicode's arrival, Hindi typists and journalists mostly used the old keyboards used by Remington typewriters, that followed a visual order for keys. They resisted the use of the new phonetic order on computer keyboards. But younger entrants into journalism learnt and used the keys adroitly. Text editing and word processing of Indic scripts remain more complex than their roman counterparts.

A lot still needs to be done to develop perfect Unicode fonts for Hindi. Even among smartphones, it is easier to type in Hindi on an iPhone than on an Android-enabled one. The automatic translation facility remains very poor. And audio facilitated typing in Hindi is still inadequate in dealing with the vital need to reproduce conjoined consonants (*sanyuktakshar*) and sound signs (*maatras* and *bindus*) in Hindi. The Apple keyboard is definitely more Hindi-friendly, but since Apple products are more expensive, most users of vernaculars cannot afford them.

'THIS IS HINDI'S EUREKA PERIOD': MEET NIDHEESH TYAGI

It is refreshing to interact with Nidheesh Tyagi on the subject of generational change and the gradual evolution of the new media in digitised Hindi. As a career journalist for nearly three decades, Tyagi, as a Chevening Fellow, studied journalism at the University of Manchester, and worked with BBC World as the head of their Hindi service. Before and after that, he worked in Delhi, Mumbai, Pune, Chandigarh, Ahmedabad, Baroda, Bhopal, Nagpur and Raipur, handling Hindi's digital, print, TV and radio avatars. He currently heads the language section at Network18 Digital, working with multiple teams in 11 languages, and employs some 250 digital journalists. He is also connected with several consultative groups that design media courses for Indian universities.

According to Tyagi (interviewed in July 2019), Hindi's entry into the internet was a sort of 'Eureka!' moment for Hindi media practitioners who felt that they were misfits in the traditional newsrooms of Hindi papers and were looking for a fresh media platform. But the average mainstream journalists did not see a bright future for digital news. Those who reported for newspapers on subjects like crime and politics, or worked at the desks monitoring news and shaping and reshaping the pages for the next day's papers, ruled the newsrooms. They felt online work offered them no space for throwing their weight about. Several who had walked out of the legacy media (print and TV news) all starry-eyed soon lost heart and chose to return. Many notable early experiments, like *Web Dunia* (technologically supported by mega companies like Microsoft) or *BBC Hindi* online, continued to progress slowly because typing on Hindi keyboards and then enabling the end user to read the content remained tedious. The tech people ruled the scene and the internet was slow. Even a slight jolt sent the websites crashing. All this required infinite patience and time, always in short supply in newsrooms.

Tyagi began his own digital innings with the Dainik Bhaskar Group (DB Corp), where, after working for a while in the Hindi and Gujarati editions of their prestigious daily *Dainik Bhaskar*, he became the first multi-media editor of the group. The parent company, DB Corp, had recently bought a digital company and he became a bridge between the print and digital sections.

After almost seven months, he says, he felt dissatisfied. The new work was not getting him anywhere, so he quit and left for Pune to start an English daily, *The Mirror*. From there, he moved to *The Tribune* of Chandigarh. By now, most major Hindi dailies like *Dainik Jagran*, *Amar Ujala* and *Dainik Bhaskar*, and major TV news channels like Aaj Tak (India Today Group) and NDTV (Hindi) had launched their digital editions. But within the system, the digital media lacked the gravitas that the print had. One reason was that the digital papers and platforms hardly generated revenue worth their name. The other reason was that most editors-in-chief had grown with the legacy media and so continued to focus their attention on their print dailies. Several of them chose to shift unwanted staff members to their digital editions and portals, where they worked mostly as coolies: carrying the news from the print editions and uploading it, in an endless loop. The budgets were small and the digital editors could not afford to commission fresh writing of a different sort for their websites, even if they wished to. The most they could do was to create a visually attractive appearance for their site and invent an almost hawker-like tone for their headlines to attract traffic. The language used was mostly unimaginative and aimed at titillating, not provoking minds into thinking. The cultural riches of Hindi lay unexplored in this digital world until some outstanding blogs began to surface.

Initially, only the very enthusiastic risk-takers from Hindi print would venture into the digital format, or a few unwanted hands from print desks. However, as the neo-literates thronged to the websites and Hindi social media created a large new public sphere for two-way communication, more professionally capable hands came into Hindi, and with that, interaction between the Hindi print and its e-papers and digital platforms underwent a sea change. Today, very often, vital news breaks first in the e-papers, which are revised 24/7, and only later in print. Those who work with the internet feel secure and more connected globally, and they are. Unlike the print and TV news that have their own pyramidal hierarchies, in digital platforms, the day's agenda is not set by some top-heavy editorial, but by the news flow. The teams are structured not vertically, but horizontally, and each worker can customise news because he has more access to various news sources.

The big traffic that began to move towards Hindi digital media in the beginning comprised of consumers in small towns in the Hindi belt, or migrants from the Hindi belt working in the new IT hubs in Mumbai, Chennai, Hyderabad and Bengaluru. Most of them worked at low level, low visibility jobs and were too poor to own their own laptops. They mostly used their office computers to 'watch' this new kind of titillating news. They loved the free news they could read at the press of a button and were not particularly interested in the quality of language or the veracity of news and information. The business technology groups within publishing houses were, however, exceedingly pleased with the sudden increase in their daily page views. Soon, success for Hindi in the digital universe was measured not by its capacity for developing and streaming fresh content or its innovative and attractive format, but by the total number of 'clicks' the site generated. The larger the number, the better the advertising potential of the platform. The marketing managers were soon handing Excel sheets with specific targets to the editorial staff. They had to show upward growth in traffic by the end of the month, or leave.

THE CONTAGIOUS DUMBING DOWN OF HINDI MEDIA

A few smart young people using digital platforms created devilishly cunning ways of registering high growth—by tabloidising their news content. It was a mixed blessing. The startling stories on black magic, superstitions and sex, Bollywood scandals, and lewd and lurid videos successfully diverted traffic to their websites. But it led to a dumbing down of the entire Hindi media, as print and TV news began to replicate their success formula. Bureaus within print, at this point, began to be seen by managers as redundant money guzzlers, so editorial teams began to be downsized. Within print, the downsizing reduced the overall budget but also shrank the space for serious, well-researched and sustained reporting, and editorial analysis of news. Interestingly, even as the headlines and tone of reporting turned sensational, many chief editors themselves shied away from upgrading their own skills in handling digital Hindi and platforms. They continued treating their e-editions as downmarket versions of the main paper, and their stories, when they were used, were mostly bunched in weekly pull-out sections. It was accepted that they titillated and added zing to the paper, and brought in more custom for city editions. But the papers' own USPs long remained firmly conjoined with the identities of their chief editors, who were largely averse to the new technology and drew strength from their ability to build bridges between the owners, major corporates and the political parties in power.

Then, around 2004–05, inexpensive smartphones arrived, and as mobile screens became connected with the internet, content began to change. The sleaze, for one, was toned down considerably since women and children also had easy access to Hindi sites. And niche news began to be created for the young and mobile users who were interested in specific areas. By now, the audiences became large enough for the editorials and managers of Hindi papers and their digital portals to start talking more knowledgeably about page views, and identifying the 'unique user' and the 'returning user'.

INTERVIEWS WITH EARLY ENTRANTS INTO THE NEW MEDIA IN HINDI

The questionnaires sent were in Hindi, as were the responses, summarised below. Translations are the author's.

Prakash Hindustani

Ex-head, Web Dunia, *the first Hindi web portal, created by the Indore-based newspaper,* Nai Dunia. *Interviewed in December 2018.*

> *Web Dunia,* interestingly, began not in the metros but in Indore, a relatively small backwater town in Madhya Pradesh. When *Web Dunia* began, Google was only a year old. And Google Plus,

Facebook, Twitter, LinkedIn, Reddit, Instagram and YouTube were not even a gleam in the eyes of their creators.

Yahoo, and in India, *Rediff.com*, both in English, led the path into the brave new world of web journalism. When I joined *Web Dunia* after working with several eminent Hindi weeklies and dailies, friends would call and ask, 'Is it true you have now become a computer operator?' It was hard to convince them that this was the gateway into an entirely new kind of journalism. During this period, what helped a bit in retaining my journalistic credentials among unbelievers was the fact that the articles I was writing for the portal were also simultaneously and regularly surfacing in the print version of *Nai Dunia*.

Vinay Chhajlaani, the grandson of media baron Labhchand Chhajlani, who launched the hugely popular newspaper, *Nai Dunia*, was the first to come up with the idea of starting a web portal in Hindi. I was his first recruit for the task. There was a long discussion; first, over the name.

Pramod Joshi

Senior journalist, ex-resident editor of the Hindi daily, Hindustan. *Interviewed in March 2018.*

The digital age entered my own life rather late, in 1998, when I was some 46 years old and working with a television channel (the Sahara group). In 1973, when I began my career with a daily (*Swatantra Bharat*) in Lucknow, the new technology was unavailable to Hindi journalists. All dailies were then composed by the hot metal technique and transmitted by teleprinters, but since the offices mostly had English teleprinters, Hindi news had to be transmitted in roman. In the 1980s, editorial pages were mostly made using the phototype setting. Those were the days when news about cricket matches being played by the Indian team in the West Indies, in the absence of the internet, became available to readers only on the third day, through the circuitous route of international telegraphic techniques, which had to take into account the time difference. Photos transmitted thus were usually poor in quality.

In the early years of the 1970s, *Nai Dunia* of Indore was the only Hindi paper using the offset printing technique. In 1982, *The Telegraph* of Kolkata was launched using the same technique. The real revolution happened around 1995, when editorial teams at Hindi papers began using digital technology and the internet. In 1985, the Aldus Corporation introduced the first version of PageMaker, mainly for the book publishing market. Then, in 1987, Microsoft Windows arrived, and in the same year, QuarkXPress was produced for Mac and Windows as software for page-making. The first fax machines arrived in Lucknow news offices around 1994–95.

The new printing technology may have been adopted by Hindi papers like *Nai Dunia* and *Dainik Jagran* before English-language newspapers, but acceptance of digital software and content in Hindi took another decade. The Hindi papers, by the 1990s, were printing in colour and gradually began shifting to using desktop computers.

In 1999, I joined the Hindustan Times Group as night editor for their Hindi daily, *Hindustan*, amid scenes of great resistance against changing technology by the old staff there. The *Hindustan Times* had by then launched its web portal in English, but the Hindi paper had no digital version. In July 1999, web journalism entered Hindi through the Indore-based *Nai Dunia* group's ambitious portal, called 'Web Dunia'. This was the first of its kind in India.

Bigger newspapers, due to intense resistance from the unions and many workers in editorial, whose work and livelihood this made obsolete, caught up later. By 2005, *Hindustan* had launched its digital site along with other major Hindi dailies, like *Navbharat Times*, *Dainik Jagran*, *Dainik Bhaskar* and *Rajasthan Patrika*. Initially, these websites were digital reproductions of the daily newspapers, not independent digital sites. That took another decade. At first, the editorial for print doubled up to feed the portal each day, some working night shifts to upload the pages that had been transmitted for printing to the print centres earlier that evening. The pages were hardly ever updated in the daytime. Many young editorial workers were excited by the development, but felt inadequate to meet the new challenge as well-trained media men and women. The older staff resisted more than the young ones, so most portals had young teams.

At that point, since there was no Unicode, we had to provide the Hindi font for our readers. We used Dongals for typing in Hindi on the regular machines, some 100 in number in our Delhi office alone. We used an editorial system called 'ALEX' but because it was created abroad, mostly for English and European languages, we had to do all kinds of jugaad to use it for Hindi and it often 'hung'. We needed better techniques for unhindered work flow, and a computer management system suited to Hindi. The first Indian company that came out with one such system was 4Cplus. Its founder, Sanjay

Gupta, was very helpful to us at *Hindustan* in developing proper Hindi fonts that rid us of the Dongal age.

Harjinder Singh

Senior journalist, ex-head of Hindustan Dainik *e-paper. Interviewed in April 2018.*

We had not imagined such a proliferation of Hindi on the internet when we began. The reason being that Hindi stood way behind in this field. There were major technical problems that were yet to be professionally tackled. Everyone agreed that digitised Hindi had a bright future but the state it was in hardly supported such positivity.

I began with the daily *Amar Ujala*'s website. At that point, there were only two major platforms on the web: *Dainik Jagran* and *Web Dunia*. *Hindustan* and *Navbharat Times* had not entered the arena, and *Dainik Bhaskar*, another major Hindi daily, had marked only a token presence for itself. Our portal had a complicated relationship with our printed paper; our team was small and it had been decided that all our content will be lifted from our newspaper. We did not have enough hands to handle the proliferation of news (some 2,000–4,000 stories daily), so we looked for technical solutions. We realised that if news was forwarded to us in a particular format, ready for the portal, we could put it all online within 2–3 hours.

It took our colleagues some time to create a web-friendly format. For around two years, until our team visited all the various centres and trained personnel, we struggled hard to stay afloat. Our more experienced and ambitious colleagues were unwilling to be connected with this new portal and when some hands were transferred to our department, they thought they were being put out to pasture.

When I was made in charge of the web edition, most colleagues, as also the managers, treated me as a technical hand, not an editorial man. One manager even ordered me to oversee the marketing of the venture.

Another problem was that our print centres continued to block exclusive stories and provided the web portal with only routine news. They did not wish to alert their rivals, they said, who might steal their exclusive stories. Most of them felt their main job was to service the newspaper. The website was a side job that had to be done.

Unicode was unavailable in those days. We used a temporary font on our site known as 'EOT' [Embedded OpenType]. We had to download it before downloading the page, which was quite time-consuming. We requested the desk at the paper to download EOT on their computers first and then the content. This took some time. Unicode came in mostly due to Windows 98, and at that point, it was not the ideal version. The Hindi papers accepted this system rather late. But once they did, our lives became easier.

Currently, a major problem we face is that unlike English, Hindi technically uses two separate fonts for the print and the internet versions. So the need for conversion has not disappeared, which takes time and increases the scope for errors.

As for the governmental use of new media technology, it is mostly done under compulsion. The proof is that on their own websites, neither their format nor their Hindi is user-friendly.

Social media has opened up vast possibilities for Hindi now. It may well be that many other languages, including English, are envious of their reach and influence among users. There are dangers, too, but they are faced by all languages, not just Hindi.

For the young, the internet is their entire existence. And as the flow of digitised Hindi is moving towards rural areas, thanks to laptops and smartphones, the young are emerging as our major consumers. Even print journalists use the World Wide Web a lot for culling and tracking news, although this has many hidden dangers.

At the moment, the news sites launched by major Hindi newspapers and news channels are in good shape. Their major strength derives from ready-to-upload content that they get from their parent organisation, the newspaper or the channel. Standalone portals and sites are in no position to compete with them. Content generation requires big money and an army of gatherers, which the latter cannot afford. However, most now seem to agree that the future of news lies with the digitised versions, so wise media owners are investing a lot in them. Those who work with the internet are no longer treated as outsiders and there is a healthy and constant interaction between both.

Nachiketa Desai

Senior journalist, ex-editor, Web Dunia, *and* Indiainfo.com, *a multi-Indian language portal. Interviewed in June 2019.*

I was associated with the first Hindi news portal, *Web Dunia*, in 1999. At that point, newspapers had not launched e-papers due to various technical problems. The newspaper, *Nai Dunia*, lent the website all the content, including news from the Press Trust of India [PTI] and the Indo-Asian News Service [IANS]. A company in Indore, Suvi Infotech, created the first portable fonts for the internet, which we used. After downloading these, readers could read the content directly on the internet. Later, the company sold this technique to Microsoft.

Soon after this, I became associated with *Indiainfo.com*, which provided content in multiple Indian languages: Hindi, Gujarati, Tamil, Telugu, Malayalam and Kannada. The team employed by the group was paid well and worked with great enthusiasm. I have worked with either the print or the web portals, but never for both simultaneously.

The Hindi media today is not generating as much content as it should. Hindi web journalists are using the internet as a source for news instead of generating fresh stories for it. The young are enthusiastic users, but they lean more towards visual content. Many young YouTubers are earning well, but standalone news websites are short of revenue that will come in only if they begin generating fresh content. It is easier for websites linked to major newspapers or channels to access stories as the print still employs large teams of news gatherers and editors. Hindi has a lot of potential that has yet to be tapped.

CONCLUSION

The latest IRS (2019b) and ABC reports confirm a steady growth of both Hindi print and digital media. Initially, Hindi newspapers entered the internet age diffidently. Interviews with early entrants show that the earliest Hindi-language entrants in the field were not metro-based, multi-language media companies, but dailies like *Nai Dunia* of Indore, whose *Web Dunia* was the first portal launched, with help from Microsoft. However, most chief editors in the first decade of the new millennium treated their e-papers and digital portals as by-products of the main print product. The young men (almost no women) who worked with the digital sections were either risk-takers or unwanted hands in the main newsrooms. Those managing e-papers just uploaded the print versions more or less as they were. The portals were not well-designed and handling hardware created to cater to roman letters and keyboards posed several operational problems for those working in Hindi or other Indian languages. Things eased after the hardware was improved by the major global companies who were keen to enter Indian markets. Interaction and editorial work flow became easier after Unicode-branded software became available in Hindi. As blogs emerged in Hindi, one saw a young generation of writers who understood the new medium and crafted their Hindi to suit it. Within a decade, as social media grew and smartphones connected people, especially women, in small towns and rural areas with the internet, a whole new media industry grew. Print remained the most regular supplier of news, especially local news, but the importance of the digital departments grew. News, by 2014, was breaking first in the internet-connected media, from where it was trawled by the print to upgrade their own news.

Two problems arose. One, the print began a process of pruning its news bureaus and desk staff. This diluted institutional memory and also weakened the time-tested methods of editorial cross-checks and verification. Two, during the 2014 general elections, all major political parties used both traditional print and social media, and found that accessing audiences and feeding them all kinds of stories was far more effective on social media. The new readers were younger and wanted their news flow to be portable, available 24/7 and exciting. To cater to them, Hindi news on the internet began breaking news with sensational headlines through the day. With that, fake news and morphed videos also surfaced on a large scale in the media. The print, keen to gather more readers and advertisers, followed suit and by the time the next general elections were announced in early 2019, consumers of Hindi news were hooked on to the constant sensationalisation of news and flamboyant political propaganda. It paid the media rich dividends in the shape of political advertising, but the media's own image took a hard knock. When the media criticised political parties' provocative speeches and majoritarianism, the latter turned around and accused the media of having sold out for money or favours to their rivals. Even senior political leaders used exceptionally crude terms to describe the liberals and intellectuals whom the media supported.

The tabloidisation of the media continues, but its rapid expansion and the recent concern shown by global media giants for intemperate language, fake news and vicious communal propaganda gives one hope that the media will tweak the medium to save their own image. The other reason to feel positive about the multi-media scene in Hindi is the emergence of a whole group of young, skilled and deft media workers who are adept at multitasking and spirited interaction with news sources. The old pyramidal structures of authority within newsrooms are gradually giving way to more horizontally structured ones, where anyone who is handling the news flow is free to take editorial decisions and rectify mistakes. What we face now is an entirely different media in which people are not passive recipients of news, but are constantly engaging with their news providers, communicating and sharing information. It is a constantly shifting world where there is growing competition for audiences, and crucially, advertising revenues. It is hard to predict a clear future for the Hindi media at this point, but one hopes that as in the early decades of the twentieth century, the sizeable Hindi-speaking area and its audience will once again push for a robust, democratic space in which they have a voice.

6

Hindi Newspapers

It is becoming customary for analysts and digital media experts to ascribe changes in the Hindi print media, especially negative ones, to the rise of digital media, which is swiftly detaching itself from its roots in print and charting its own course. India may be one of the world's fastest growing markets, but recent data shows that all media are growing simultaneously, some more than others, but yes, all are growing. Hindi newspapers are still one of the most profitable segments in India's media scene.

The Audit Bureau of Circulations, a Mumbai-based non-profit organisation, has been certifying circulation figures for most of India's large publishing houses since 1948. According to its May 2017 report (ABC 2017), between 2006 and 2016, the print media saw a 23.7 million rise in circulation (a compounded annual growth rate of 4.87 per cent). And this happened despite the stiff competition print faced from television, radio and the fast-growing digital media industry.

A study by KPMG and Google (2017) confirmed that the Indian language internet user base grew by 41 per cent between 2011 and 2016 to touch 234 million, with a projected growth rate of 18 per cent. So, digital vernacular-language media may be taking its user numbers to 536 million by 2021. If that happens, by 2021, the Indian language users of the internet, the study predicts, will form 75 per cent of the total internet user base in India. Analysts are pegging this growth at 'moderate adoption levels'.

So far, media growth in India, as columnist Vanita Kohli-Khandekar (2019b) suggests, remains 'supplementary, not cannibalistic'. United by the internet, but divided by the format, the legacy and the new digital media are together producing a varied bouquet. As is inevitable, all the various segments are also facing a Darwinian struggle, where ultimately the fittest in each genre shall survive.

Table 6.1   Number of Print Outlets in India, 2018

Media outlet	Number
Registered publications	118,239
Periodicals	21,187
Monthlies	6,138
Weeklies	10,834
Dailies	8,930

Source: Registrar of Newspapers for India (2019: 15).

DAINIK JAGRAN: HOW A STRONG HINDI PRINT PRODUCT MESHED WITH DIGITAL MEDIA

In the 2010s, the demographically rich Hindi heartland had a surge in income and literacy rates, and consumers realised the importance of information. And they were ready to buy their Hindi newspapers at a per copy price that is substantially higher than that of the English dailies.

A complete newspaper in the Hindi belt still means one which covers local as well as national and international news, alongside subjects that engage with the needs of the entire family, including women and children. To satisfy them, all major Hindi dailies, which had earlier inserted a weekly page on 'soft' subjects, today bring out various supplements through the week. These focus on information about various careers and the latest gadgets for the young, stories, games and puzzles for children, fashion and lifestyle news for younger women, and religion and astrology-based articles for the elderly.

The Hindi reader in a small town is ambitious and upwardly mobile. He realises the importance of English as a social marker and as an asset for getting jobs with higher salaries, but while he picks up the language in college and in English language classes, his daily Hindi paper remains his friend, philosopher and guide. The apps on his smartphone with a Hindi keyboard facility connect him to the World Wide Web, and through this, this reader can access digitised information of various kinds. In the last two decades, supplements have focused on this young, aspirational group of readers keen to enter their English-speaking, upwardly mobile peer groups. The supplements, therefore, use English terms copiously in their headlines and also when talking of new trends in cookery, home décor, and make-up and fashion.

The Jagran Prakashan Group, the market leader among newspapers in Hindi, is proof of the above phenomenon. Its flagship publication, *Dainik Jagran*, headquartered in Kanpur, is published from 13 print locations and has a total readership of 70 million. It has over 400 editions and sub-editions. And according to information provided in its 2018 annual report (Jagran Prakashan 2018), the Jagran Group now claims a readership base of over 84 million for its 10 print products.

In addition to print, the Jagran Group also owns 39 radio stations across 12 states. It also has 11 digital media portals, of which the one in the Hindi news, information, and education category is the number one Hindi portal in that category.

In 2017–18, the Jagran Group earned Rs 1,697 crore as ad revenue. The revenue from sales is listed as Rs 433 crore. The break-up of revenue figures provided are as follows: *Dainik Jagran*, 65 per cent; other print publications, 15 per cent; radio, 13 per cent; events and outdoor ads, 6 per cent; and digital, 1 per cent (ibid.: 6–7).

Dainik Bhaskar: Another Major Hindi Daily That Chose to Flaunt Print's Traditional Credibility in the Hindi Belt

The second most popular daily (often claiming to be the first), *Dainik Bhaskar*, belongs to DB Corp. They launched their Hindi paper from Bhopal in 1958 and began to grow around 1996, after launching an edition in Rajasthan. By 2019, they were publishing a total of 63 editions in 14 states, mainly in Hindi but also in Gujarati, Marathi and English. In June 2017, *Dainik Bhaskar*, boosted by the success of its e-paper, went on to launch its own news app on three different platforms: Android, iPhone and Windows.

Navneet Gurjar (interviewed in August 2019), who heads the *Dainik Bhaskar* digital team, is optimistic about the future of digitised news in Hindi. He believes that most digital platforms of Hindi dailies are still trying to woo audiences below 30 years of age. This has resulted in the unwarranted trivialisation of news and a debasement of language that eventually impacts the credibility of their news. This audience, he predicts, will soon age and want a more sober news package. At *Dainik Bhaskar*, they try, as far as possible, to select their news carefully and apply time-tested standards from print to judge the veracity of information, and use proper formatting. In their hurry to chase young audiences, Gurjar says, digitised Hindi platforms forget that ultimately, it is the trust between the reader and the product that matters more than raciness of language and content.

Gurjar also believes that in matters of revenue gathering, print will always attract more than the digital media. The best revenue model for the digital media in Hindi, therefore, must be subscription-based.

In the age of aggregated news apps and the steady expansion of the internet, with the announcement of a hike of 10 per cent for the import of newsprint in 2019, the print arm of *Dainik Bhaskar* realised that though it is growing, it faces tough competition from the online media, which is attracting traffic from college-going youth, diverting them steadily away from print. So, it came up with an advertising campaign with the Bollywood film superstar, Salman Khan, asking Hindi readers, 'What if your morning tea were to be delivered in a golden cup? [*Agar aapki subah ki chai sone ke cup mein aaye toh?*] Life will change, boss!'

Dainik Bhaskar posted a growth in revenue of 6.2 per cent in 2018–19, with a 7.4 per cent growth in its ad revenues (DB Corp 2019: 10). In the months before the 2019 elections, it took a proactive stand on behalf of the print media and brought together three other major newspaper groups, *The Times of India* (which also publishes the Hindi daily *Navbharat Times*), *Hindustan Times* (with its Hindi daily, *Hindustan*) and *The Hindu*. The ad agency Famous Innovations created a full-page joint ad (claiming to be pro bono), which ran in the papers published by all four groups. The ad highlighted the comparative superiority of print news, claiming that all the news in these newspapers underwent disciplined fact-checking, as opposed to online news, which deleted and edited their news regularly. *Dainik Bhaskar* ran this jacket ad in 12 markets.

A Look at the Internet Explosion, 2014–18

How did the upsurge of 65 per cent in internet usage between 2014 and 2018 come about in Hindi? A major push came from the easier availability of inexpensive laptops (often freely distributed by governments to college-going voters, mostly as election freebies). Next came the growth in the number of inexpensive smartphones that flooded the Indian market. In this hugely competitive market, telecom operators began swiftly to drop tariffs for smartphone users. Jio, the Mukesh Ambani-owned Reliance group's service provider, took it to new heights when it introduced the mind-boggling inaugural offer of free connectivity for an initial period. This racked up 100 million subscribers for Jio in just 170 days. Reliance also introduced 4G connectivity, pushing the growth of smartphone app users further. This was a boon for apps like Twitter and Facebook, which has since gone on to acquire other popular messaging apps, like WhatsApp (in February 2014).

For Hindi today, Twitter, Facebook and Instagram have emerged as the most favoured and sought-after social media platforms. Together, they have created a whole new kind of Hindi news consumer. And as gatekeepers of most people's information diets, their regularly updated newsfeeds drive news traffic in all Indian languages in the smallest towns and rural areas.

The Indian Readership Survey (MRUC 2019a), the world's largest face-to-face multi-media and consumption study, makes three important points about India's internet users for the first quarter of 2019:

1. Active internet users in India have grown significantly: 24 per cent of total universe.
2. Rural India now accounts for 50 per cent of active internet users.
3. Every second person in urban India today is an internet user.

What Swift Digitisation and Internet Penetration has Meant for Hindi Print

For the legacy media, digitisation has helped them scour vast tracts of news flowing in from social media and other sources. For the teams, it has helped to spot and suggest stories to be reported or chased, to personalise and localise news for various devices, and make the accurate automation of repeatable events (elections, natural disasters, mishaps or political speeches) possible. But this has had serious long-term implications for professional journalists:

1. It is fast making the task of collecting, sifting, arranging and disseminating news almost entirely mechanical, leading to staff downsizing.
2. The need for local reporting has also become more acute, as Hindi media reaches the rural heartland. This has also led to an increasing reliance on often untrained freelancers (who are cheap and willing).
3. It has strengthened Hindi media's reliance on ready-to-use feeds and the fierce competition to be the first in the market with the latest news, but led to the weakening of control over vital cross-checking and verification. This has often resulted in fake and planted news flooding the media and going viral before it is weeded out.
4. Field reporting in Hindi today is now provided increasingly by young freelancers armed with smartphones with cameras. They send their reports directly to the 24/7 digital platforms linked to all major Hindi newspapers, where they are sifted and prioritised by the digital staff.

Due to this, there is a swell in the number of news items and video feeds available through the day, but the news flow is often so fast that crucial checking and editing is not exercised as it should be.

The Evolving Structure of Hindi Newspapers and Survival Strategies for Reporters

In an atmosphere such as this, constant innovation and upgrading of reporters' skills is the key to survival. With the average reader/

consumer getting younger and more demanding, innovations in tailoring content and design, and devising proper work flow systems are necessary. The age of popular small local dailies is all but over. Papers like *Nai Dunia* are often being bought (*Nai Dunia* is now a part of the Jagran group) and merged with the regional editions of mega dailies.

Some things remain unchanged so far. Despite the rise in newsprint costs, on average, the main book retains a 16–20 page broadsheet format. And the cover cost remains one-sixth of the real cost of production per copy. This means huge cross-subsidies from ad revenues and ceding more and more space to 'creatives' (mostly imaginatively created visuals that leap at you from each page), where ads imitate the editorial layout. The ratio between edit space and advertising was expected to be around a 60:40 ratio, so it can give readers some 90 columns of news every day in an eight-column grid paper. But it is common now during the festive season or elections for Hindi papers to devote the entire front (and often the reverse page too) to full-page ads. On lean days, the edit space break-up is usually 30 per cent of space for local news, 30 per cent for national and international news, 30 per cent for sports, business and technology, and 10 per cent for edit, op-edit, opinion.

Supplements are an area where business and content issues may vary from market to market. Infotainment, Bollywood, lifestyle, home, education and careers are the usual areas covered; research and digital 'likes' have revealed newer areas like healthcare/wellness, computers and travel. Lately, news generated by social media and Hinduism have been occupying more and more space in print. Innovation in structure and page numbers in Hindi still requires a nod and suggestions from the space-selling and distribution teams far more often than their English sister dailies, most of whom have editorial members who report directly to the owner-editors.

Readership Research

Except for the ABC or IRS lists, there is little available to Hindi editorials by way of credible area-wise data that may systematically indicate Hindi readership preferences. Hindi papers, until the global media giants began meticulously researching Hindi readership patterns, relied mostly on the anecdotal wisdom of old managers and dealers, informed gossip and managers' perceptions of what new readers want based on what they gleaned from the internet. With the new ownership patterns, many crucial decisions in Hindi newsrooms about prioritisation of information, political news in particular, are increasingly linked now to what newsrooms refer to as 'orders from above'. This may mean orders from the CEO, or filtered versions of orders from the owners who may have received a phone call from a government ministry or some important functionary from the media cell of a powerful political party that monitors Hindi media closely.

Traditionally, Hindi newspapers created their pages at or close to each centre of publication. Technology gradually facilitated centralised page-making. This saved manpower costs and duplication of effort. So now, national news pages are created mostly at a centralised location and transmitted to all locations. Local teams will mostly generate L (local) pages and customise the rest. Business and sports pages seldom need local customisation, given the perennial paucity of financial journalists.

The lack of foreign correspondents likewise keeps Hindi papers from developing their own perspectives on the reporting and analysis of global events (unless one of their favoured journalists is chosen to accompany an important minister or the prime minister). Reports filed show that in such cases, Hindi correspondents show a marked inclination to stick to the version of events provided to them by the media handlers of the government.

Opinion pages are usually made centrally. Letters to the editor and op-edit pieces are replaced at the local level. There has been a marked increase in ministers from the present-day cabinet writing editorial pieces for major Hindi dailies, especially around events relating to their own ministries. This is a bit of a change, but cosmetic mostly. Previous governments seldom graced Hindi publications with such writing from top decision-makers. Most such pieces publicise the achievements of the government, and in particular, the prime minister. Signed editorials by major cabinet ministers in various Hindi dailies on the birthday of their leader were all prominently and reverentially displayed. Given how much the poor in the Hindi states depend on the state's largesse, for the Hindi papers, a declaration straight from the Centre about the government's successful schemes, with themes woven around the poor, becomes their unique selling point.

Features teams work centrally. Locations usually have some dedicated staff for local customisation and creation of features. Good pull-outs need a good central design department with good designers, infographic artists and illustrators, and this is still missing in Hindi editorials. The results are obvious in the look and feel of the product. Women remain scarce in newsrooms in Hindi, but features sections are where they are often sedimented in clutches. Most writing they generate revolves around the usual domestic issues: food, childcare, care for the elderly, lifestyle, make-up, etc.

NEWS GATHERING AND THE INTERFACE BETWEEN HOUSE PRINT DAILIES AND THEIR MULTI-MEDIA PLATFORMS

News gathering remains the most expensive part of a news establishment and has undergone severe paring and cuts in the 2010s. PTI English and Hindi and Asian News International (ANI) are agencies used by most Hindi papers. Many houses encourage their Hindi papers to use the English agency copy only. Apart from their own photographers, they use the photo services of Agence France-Presse (AFP), Associated Press (AP), Reuters, PTI and United News of India (UNI). Graphic news, comics, puzzles, astrological forecasts and weather graphics are mostly relegated to young new hands to monitor.

The interviews with digital media heads in Chapter 5 make it clear how the earlier dependence model is changing in Hindi multi-media groups. Today, it is mostly the core teams of the digital media that collects, distils and prioritises news through the day and sends it to the print teams. Unlike the print teams, they function less in pyramidal hierarchies and more horizontally. By the evening, when the print arms begin to receive news reports from their field correspondents and stringers from other states, districts, subdivisional headquarters and rural areas, they stir into action and share these with the multi-media teams. The digital teams then update their earlier items or upload new ones after reorganising them. Blogs, Facebook and Twitter are also constantly explored for news breaks. The websites undergo several big updates through the day depending on the news flow, with the last major spurt usually around the time the print edition is sent to press.

Most Hindi dailies have by now trained their field reporters and stringers in videography through handheld mobile devices. These video logs (vlogs) are regularly streamed. However, many of them also remain unused as there is a greater preference for live videos of natural disasters and major accidents among digital audiences.

The digital editions of Hindi dailies have also taken to regularly uploading links to their special stories and news breaks on Facebook and Twitter. This attracts vital traffic from these popular social media websites to the e-papers. Some Hindi dailies initially experimented with forming special WhatsApp groups for the purpose of driving social media viewers' attention to their sites, but that has now been largely discontinued.

TRAINING

To create an outstanding product, all processes need to be streamlined. For digital media, the earlier lively combination of writing, editing and design is slowly being replaced by the new triad of digitally-driven crawling, indexing and retrieval. The exercises, however, call for proper orientation and training. Senior team members are required to align their vision so it percolates down to the incumbents. But as the interviews in Chapter 5 with the digital teams showed, like baby penguins, most seasoned hands were pushed into the new medium a decade ago and expected to swim.

Given the socio-economic and scholastic background of the average worker in Hindi media, only constant training and interaction with various agencies doing innovative work in the fields of technology and content generation can bring about the cultural change needed. The best hands in these areas are those who have been fortunate enough to get scholarships to go to good media schools abroad, get good degrees or attend short, but focused training courses.

Most senior journalists in Hindi today are not products of highly rated journalism schools. The schools of Hindi journalism have not yet acquired the proper faculties and infrastructure required to train students for the integrated use of both old and new journalism. The available journalism and mass communication training for Hindi media needs vast correctional efforts. As the interviews showed us, there is no clash of interest between new professionals and the old guard, but technologically, every day something new emerges and new media platforms are born. Success may come in unexpected ways.

Since 2016, Google, in partnership with DataLEADS and Internews, has been training people in 30 Indian cities in online verification and fact-checking techniques. They have, as of 2019, trained 13,000 men and women. All three major players in social media—Facebook, Google and Twitter—have also promised to intensify checks on political advertising on their platforms.

Hindi for Policy Propagation

Unlike its rivals, the National Democratic Alliance (NDA) government has understood the importance of the Hindi media for winning friends and influencing people in the demographically richest region of twenty-first century India. The Hindi belt was gradually charmed or coerced, through the government's sympathisers in the Hindi media industry, into supporting Narendra Modi's candidature for prime ministership in 2014, and again in 2019. However, the new government in 2014 gradually created a whole new template for interaction between the media and the Prime Minister's Office. It shunned bonhomie and intimate interaction of any sort, the kind that had earlier produced exclusive interviews and stories. Senior members of the cabinet and bureaucrats were explicitly instructed to refrain from maintaining one-on-one contact with the media. Notes and agenda papers, freely available to the much-lionised English media earlier, all but ceased to find their way into their hands. And routine but important media briefings by the prime minister have since become rare affairs.

Prime ministerial communication with the media since 2014 has been more or less one-sided. The preferred mode seems to be a popular social media service like Twitter. According to the information available on the PMO's website in August 2019, Modi has 49.5 million followers. And his personal accounts and mobile app also show a further 2.2 million followers.

The other communication channel used by the prime minister on a regular basis is the public service broadcaster, All India Radio, which broadcasts a monthly programme, *Mann ki Baat*, in which the prime minister talks directly to Indians in Hindi about subjects ranging from building toilets, getting their daughters to school and helping women with household chores. He has also begun to speak emphatically on environmental matters and the need to conserve wildlife and the planet. On Independence Day 2019, the globally renowned Discovery Channel aired a documentary of the prime minister's rambles through the forest in Jim Corbett National Park with the well-known adventurer Bear Grylls (*Man vs. Wild* 2019). This show, in which Modi spoke only in Hindi, received wide coverage in the Hindi media, despite the fact that Grylls spoke only English. The prime minister later explained to audiences in one of his speeches how comprehension was facilitated during the trip using a new device for real-time translation from Hindi to English.

THE 2019 ELECTORAL CAMPAIGN

The 2014 elections are an interesting case study for media students. The electoral rallies carefully constructed an image of the BJP leader as a man of humble origins, an indefatigable crusader against corruption and a symbol of Hindu masculinity. In addition to this, 3D images of the leader were used during his addresses to rallies in far-off corners of India, while digital messaging services carried the party's and his message to all those who could be reached through the internet (*BBC News* 2014). It helped that smartphones, launched a little earlier, made rural audiences accessible in a way that was inconceivable in the 2010 elections. All this seems to have gone down very well with media consumers, particularly in the backward and poverty-riddled states in the Hindi heartland. The poll results from the Hindi heartland revealed that people by and large saw Modi as a clean and positive role model and a great promoter of their mother tongue, Hindi.

The practices used in 2014 were further honed and perfected by the BJP in the 2019 elections. In a comprehensive paper published in *The India Forum*, a journal magazine on contemporary issues, senior journalist Sevanti Ninan (2019) quotes Amit Malviya, head of the

BJP's media cell, telling the *Economic Times* that the 2019 elections would be fought on mobile phones and that they could be dubbed as India's 'WhatsApp elections'.

Early in 2019, Hindi news channel NaMo TV was launched on YouTube. It telecast Modi's speeches and electoral rallies non-stop. It was carried a little later on direct-to-home platform Tata Sky, which merely described it as a free special services channel (*The Wire* 2019). It disappeared when the electoral process ended and has not been seen since.

A similar channel, Tiranga TV, also came into being around the same time. It promoted the Congress party and its leadership and one of the major promoters was a Congress member. It has also been more or less discontinued and is seen occasionally running old programmes in a digital format.

FIRST QUARTER AD REVENUES ACROSS MEDIA FIRMS POST 2019 ELECTIONS

A report on 21 August 2019 in the financial daily *Business Standard* (Kohli-Khandekar 2019b) revealed that the first quarter revenues for 2019 were seen declining across all media firms that publish the highest selling Hindi dailies. HT Media, which publishes the Hindi daily *Hindustan Dainik*, reported a total shortfall of 9 per cent, and DB Corp, one of the largest language media groups in the country (publisher and owner of *Dainik Bhaskar*, several digital brands and 30 radio stations among them), reported a shortfall of 2.8 per cent. Even the market leader in Hindi, *Dainik Jagran* (whose company Jagran Prakashan owns brands in print, digital and radio), showed a loss of 3.2 per cent in its total ad revenues.

It is true that in the last four decades, disposable incomes in small-town India have risen and the great Chinese Wall between English and vernacular publications has begun to crumble. And almost all chief editors of Hindi media publications are the sons of previous editors, but are far smarter and more market savvy. Like the new media barons, the vernacular readers, who themselves grew up on a diet of language papers, have children who went to English-medium schools. These brave new bilingual households of the future could be the new focus area, since this is where the action is, but the growth areas for

Hindi remain among the first-gen literates studying in government-run Hindi-medium schools in the vast Hindi belt. Most of them voted for the right-wing majoritarian parties this time (see Ninan 2019).

Advertising, no matter which political party or coalition of parties is voted to power, remains a major tool of the corporates and the government to control the media. The Government of India, a great promoter of Hindi, reportedly planned to spend as much as Rs 2.13 crore for Hindi and Rs 1.41 crore on the English media. It also significantly enhanced the ad rates (by 11 per cent) for print and private news channels that are supportive of its policies. Transparent and independent coverage of content gets compromised a great deal by way of such 'soft pressure ... to articulate the point of view of the government in a contentious issue' (Reporters without Borders and DataLEADS 2019b).

Senior journalist Raksha Kumar, in a story published in August 2019 points out that the Hindi media, catering to small-town and rural India, is also coping with a deep rot within, which stems from print's increasing obsession with ad revenues from these areas even as its large urban sources begin to dry up. She quotes a 38-year-old stringer from UP working simultaneously for four major Hindi dailies, who is forced to spend more and more time on soliciting advertising and less and less on news gathering. It shows, she writes, that while people's sources of news are changing from print to mobile phones, if the Indian print media is to survive with dignity as a professional source of news, it must urgently change its decaying nuts and bolts. The problem is largely systemic, which is getting worse due to extraneous socio-political factors. Improving the poor media literacy in the Hindi heartland and arranging for proper technology training for staff are the needs of the hour for the Hindi media. The English media may remain the voice of the movers and shakers in Delhi and metro towns, but the media needs of the real India that votes for democracy must be addressed in this age of feeble opposition parties, the weakening rupee and increasing centralisation of power.

The Strange Case of a State Government Inviting Paid News

The government of Jharkhand, one of the states slated to go to the polls in 2019, had, through an advertisement inserted in the papers by its information and public relations department, asked all journalists in the state to submit proposals for 'positive' reports about the government (Kislaya 2019). After 30 of the best journalists had been selected by a specially created committee, they had to, within 30 days, do the story and submit it to the competent government authority. After being scrutinised, they then had to get it published, telecast, broadcast or uploaded onto a digital platform. Each creator was to receive a payment of Rs 15,000 per piece from the department. Similarly, 25 articles were to be selected for inclusion in a publicity booklet to be published by the government, for which each writer was to be given 'honour money' (*maan dhan*) to the tune of Rs 5,000 per item. The journalists, however, were responsible for getting their story published and all video and print reports had to be vetted by the government.

BOUNDARIES AND FIREWALLS AROUND EDITORIALS UNDER STRESS AS FAKE NEWS STREAMS IN

In 1985, Princeton professor Harry G. Frankfurt published a short essay on the phenomenon of fake news. Only, he called it 'bullshit'. His theory was that when an honest man speaks, he says only what he believes to be true; for the liar, however, lies are correspondingly indispensable. He knows his statement is untrue. The bullshitter goes further. For him, all bets are off. In a multilingual, multicultural society, over-reliance on digital content providers can be a cause for worry because as the firewalls around editorials disappear, the field is further cleared for bullshitters (excerpted in Coombes 2017).

Around the 2004 general elections, fake or 'planted' news began to be visible in many Hindi dailies across the heartland. Over the coming years, a devilishly cunning scheme was launched by some marketing folks associated with an English daily. Their philosophy seemed to be that since various interested parties paid their news gatherers for favourable mentions in their media space, why should they, the paper, not declare such insertions formally, charge a definite fee and sign special agreements with willing companies and individuals to promote them as a brand and occasionally deny space to their perceived rivals?

Others soon followed this pattern and by the end of the first decade of the new millennium, the venerable Press Council of India (PCI), alarmed by the growth of paid news, appointed a two-member committee in 2010 to look into the malaise.

The Press Council Report on Paid News

The committee's meticulously researched report (PCI 2011) concluded that paid news as it stood reflected the warped priorities of India's corporatised media, and that a large section routinely released paid-for information under the guise of independent and objective news. As an organised phenomenon, this made paid news, now masked under many legal layers, near intractable. And several lawyers and lawmakers were complicit in the creation of this phenomenon.

News of the report was slated to be released by mid-July of the same year, but its release was deferred due to strong protests from its members, many of whom were major publishers themselves. They felt that as it stood, the report could destroy the publishers' credibility in the market. Towards the end of the year, a shorter version of the report was published with the names of the biggest alleged perpetrators, many of whom headed the major media houses. Later, a popular weekly obtained the report by filing a right to information (RTI) request and published it in its entirety.

It is noteworthy that on 3 May 2013, under advice from the Election Commission of India (ECI), the Supreme Court ruled that if any candidate suppressed their expenditure on advertising while campaigning and was found guilty of having had paid news inserted on their behalf, they would be disqualified under Section 10A of the Representation of the People Act, 1951 (Anand 2014). In 2011, in the case of one Umlesh Yadav, an elected MLA from Bisauli in Uttar Pradesh, when the PCI approached the Election Commission on the grounds that at least two major Hindi dailies in UP had published advertisements for this candidate that were not mentioned in the list of election expenses filed, the ECI, after investigation, disqualified her from contesting any election for three years (Balaji 2011). Nearly a decade later, media laws regarding ownership and responsibility remain fragmented, incoherent. And litigating against offenders is a long, time-consuming and money-guzzling prospect.

A sting operation was carried out in 2018 by independent group *Cobrapost*, with one of its undercover reporters posing as one Acharya Atal. Named Operation 136, the sting operation, it was claimed, had surreptitiously recorded employees from 17 major media houses agreeing to plant stories for a fee ranging from Rs 6 crore to Rs 50 crore, which would go on to polarise the targeted audience and malign certain political leaders (Banerji 2018). Only two English dailies published the report. One major Hindi daily whose correspondent was named therein moved the courts swiftly against the report and had the exposé blocked.

In the new millennium, Frankfurt's bullshitter (see Coombes 2017) has his task cut out as a steady unapologetic creator of fake news for the Indian public.

CONCLUSION

The global media has come a long way, from Gutenberg to Zuckerberg. New technology has facilitated global flow of news 24/7, and India is no exception. Our mobile revolution began in real terms around 2014 when various government decisions and fierce competition in the market among service providers led to a boom in the sales of inexpensive smartphones and very low tariffs. As the young, both in rural and urban India, took to digitised media in the vernacular, the Hindi media scene underwent a quick change. The market leaders that had already launched e-papers also started web portals and linked their digital teams, and with their help connected their readers to various sources of 24/7 news through apps and popular websites like Facebook, YouTube and the Chinese video portal, TikTok.

Today, these major global aggregators are becoming vital news sources for Hindi readers. Media houses, now denied proximity to the political party in power and ministerial press conferences, are busy finding new ways of generating exclusive interactions with the government and the intellectual classes through annual meets, seminars, literary festivals and melas.

This has caused the old-style newsroom arrangements to change and power is fast shifting from print to multi-media. Power structures within papers are no longer pyramidal but horizontal. News breaks happen first in the digital space and find their way into the print newsrooms only at the end of the day. To cut costs, papers in India are also pruning their print newsrooms, and while it is good to clear out redundant staff, this is also causing a major loss in institutional memory and pragmatism that came with years of handling news. The brisk 24/7 news streams are not adequately fact-checked, and at the behest of the owner-editors, there is an unspoken emphasis on carrying the government's opinions more prominently and playing down inconvenient facts. The stress has turned most staff, from senior editorial members to village stringers, into service managers whose primary job is not news gathering but advertising.

The government, for its part, is fully aware of the importance of Hindi for carrying its message to every last village. It has developed astute media policies whereby the government-controlled audio-visual media, as also privately owned TV news and print, have become spokespersons for the government. The strategy has paid rich dividends for both the government and the media houses that supported its political campaigning in the 2019 elections. The government now carefully chooses when it will address the media and how, and also which newspapers and channels shall be barred from receiving coveted government advertising for being overly critical of their policies.

This has impacted the Hindi media in two major ways. One, editorial acumen has been diluted and revenue growth has become more important for the boardrooms. This has dimmed the boundaries between editorial teams and the markets further, and prevented the usual frank and transparent coverage of elections in all their multi-tiered unfurling. Two, paid news has staged a comeback along with a bigger demon: fake news. Fake news has proliferated because the earlier checks and balances have been weakened and new ones for monitoring and cross-checking digital news and videos have yet to be perfected.

Training staff to handle multi-media is very important at this juncture. But while giants like Google, Facebook and Twitter are trying to promote fact-checking websites and creating tools to flag real news from fake, owners of Hindi media are not seen to be doing much except allowing their staff to occasionally attend workshops on digital media and its tools.

This indifference to routine skill upgradation, and rebuilding motivated and skilled editorial teams is beginning to take a toll on revenues—in the first and second quarter results of 2019, Hindi media giants recorded a small but worrisome drop in revenue.

If print is to survive new challenges, and utilise and strengthen their digital arms at the same time, it must pay heed to replacing its rusty nuts and bolts, plug the breaches in its multi-media editorials, and allow the system to function along professional lines.

7

The New Media Ecology

There is a slow realisation in the world today that similarity of technology does not automatically lead to a uniformly similar global media. Nor will it create consumers who are equally well informed. This is not to say that globalisation has not helped humanity. But of late, there have been clear signs of growing inequalities, both within and between societies, that are often driven by new devices and technical platforms on offer. The top of the pyramid belongs almost entirely to the developed nations that have created the new media giants, and are the biggest beneficiaries of the technological revolution. And in the process, they have unwittingly eliminated the economic powers and political value of other, less developed nations and societies.

For developing nations like India, the linkages between telecommunication and development have been vital for growth. But a perceptible divide remains between users of English and the vernaculars. Our currency may be carried in 16 Indian languages, but both the state and the society that legitimise and legislate on media bodies and privately owned media structures (devices used, communication activities and practices) continue to function along caste, gender, linguistic and communal hierarchies. This complex system denies equality of media access to several groups, in defiance of a Constitution that promises equality to all. Such (largely overlooked) socio-political arrangements and organisational forms muffle voices from the margins, and impede access and free interaction with the media for women, minorities, Dalits and tribals, most of whom can use only the vernaculars.

This fact is especially worth underscoring because political power equations in India have changed drastically in the years since 2014 due to new mobile telephony and the internet. The deeper and faster diffusion of information drives traffic towards the vernaculars in the mediascape, but most new consumers are unaware of the ability of social media to connect people and causes that interest them, which is especially useful for disempowered groups in finding mentors and political processes of consequence. Nor do they know about the importance of privacy laws and that certain human hands may be operating within the infrastructure, driving their minds and needs to benefit parties within the political arena or the markets. So content becoming available in Hindi needs to be accepted with more caution and less cheer.

> Content is increasingly being developed in the various regional languages.... The use of vernacular content online is estimated to increase from 45 per cent in 2013 to more than 60 per cent by 2018. The other assumptions of older media ... have also been challenged ... with media messages flowing both horizontally and vertically.... [S]ome of the characteristics of new media are interactivity, speed, simulation, connectivity, convergence, and mobility and to coin a new term 'instantaneity' (Sen Narayan and Narayanan 2016: 9–10).

This chapter is an effort to sum up new trends and examine the ways in which media systems are tackling these challenges.

IS THE SMARTPHONE A DISRUPTOR OF THE STATUS QUO?

In 2013, excited by the growth of mobiles in India, Robin Jeffrey and Assa Doron (2013: 13–14) noted, 'Pressure of ideas and economics has nudged India.... This is where the disruptive potential of the mobile phone becomes significant: the new tool affords the possibility of escaping existing structures.'

But in the five years since they wrote this, the digital world remains a field where many of the old inequalities and biases regarding caste, gender and religion seem largely intact. The vision of the inventor of the World Wide Web, of an 'open platform that allows anyone to share information, access opportunities and collaborate across geographical boundaries' (Tim Berners-Lee, quoted in Solon 2017), is being tweaked regularly by powerful digital gatekeepers and master manipulators, including many top corporates and political parties. Customer data is a vital focus area for the rich and powerful today. And there are operators who can customise the data for a fee and provide vital information and analysis about customer behaviour and also their levels of creativity, their concepts of beauty and their understanding of various health-related issues. Companies may use various methods to acquire media users' data—directly (by asking customers) or indirectly (by tracking them). There are also known instances of covert purchasing of data by political parties and global corporates from data brokers.

Roopa Kudva and Madhav Tandon (2019) of Omidyar Network India, in their article, 'An E-commerce Blueprint for India's "Next Half Billion"', reveal how the commercial world may be looking at data available from the vernacular media:

> By 2022, half a billion Indians are expected to come online through their mobile phones.... Their internet journey starts with them gaining internet access, then moving forward step by step to eventually making commercial transactions online.... They have very different income profiles, education levels, language skills and social/cultural milieus.... [E-commerce for this group] will be intent and 'impulse driven';... [it will] make product discovery easier by offering a curated selection;... leverage influencers and social media;... use Hinglish and Indic languages ... and use the viral nature of content and social media platforms to drive customer acquisition.

There you have it! Twenty-first century digital journalism in Hindi may have begun to acquire an independent face, but the real scale and long-term implications of this for the print and TV media are yet to be understood and formally recorded and analysed. One thing is sure—that there is an intensification in the race for hits and eyeballs among advertisers and corporates in the Hindi belt. It is ironic that while average young Hindi media consumers in small towns and villages are becoming more interested in splurging on personal possessions, unlike their parents, they remain stubbornly unwilling to pay for news despite an increase in interaction with the media, especially the digital Hindi media.

The need to retain a large customer base promotes the need for ads. Ads are used to keep cover prices low by cross-subsidising print, and also to launch free digital portals. This has led to the tabloidisation of Hindi print, which is getting more urban-centric, sensation-seeking and promotive of majoritarian views on caste, culture and modes of social interaction. The real issues that face our democracy and affect the lives of fellow citizens—jobs, land and mining rights, farm pricing, farmers' suicides, poor civic infrastructure, environmental pollution and increase in crime, especially against women and children—are mentioned only if they are sensational, or are promoted prior to major elections, after being endowed with a particular slant by parties that promise both political and monetary benefits.

Meanwhile, the consumption of online news jumped from 0.8 gigabytes per person per month in 2016 to 8 gigabytes by 2018, and print's share in the total media revenue has begun to decline (from 30 per cent to just over 18 per cent). This is led by an uptick in online media (IRS 2019 recorded over 279 million people reading news online) (Kohli-Khandekar 2019a). With the IRS being universally adopted by 2019, the total readership of online and offline news should eventually give a nice bump to ad revenues, especially to the top 20 online publishers in India. Will this situation prove the old adage, about bad money driving out the good, correct?

THE CORE COMPETENCIES OF THE MULTI-MEDIA INDUSTRY IN HINDI

News still remains largely situated within and linked to the mainstream print media outfits, but news streaming through Hindi social media portals and e-papers has begun to impact the 'national conversation' much more than print. As this truth seeps in, print has begun copying its rival. This means a visible shrinkage of space for reporting on vital issues missing in social media: race, immigration, policies on food, water and power distribution, and reproductive rights. The 'reshaped' print is not only allowing the Hindi readers' gender, caste, class and family biases to go unchallenged, but under pressure from its political mentors, it is also strengthening them. The readers chasing free Hindi news remain mostly unaware that free interactivity comes at a price. Their vital consumer data is being collected in the cloud somewhere and each click creates algorithmic patterns that herd them towards certain areas of tailored information, further excluding vital information that could help them become more democratically aware citizens.

THE ETHICS OF THE NEW MEDIA

A 2019 report on direct-to-home (DTH) operators (Agarwal 2019) said that after TRAI implemented the new hiked tariffs in April 2019, DTH service operators lost 18 million subscribers, reaching 55 million subscribers at the end of June 2019 (that is, a total audience of 836 million). The largely anecdotal analysis that filled the media thereafter suggested that this was an inevitable occurrence, heralding the death of revenues for print. In a scenario where three quarters of the world's digital revenues are controlled by the 'Big Two', Facebook and Twitter (Aryan 2021), what remained largely unreported was the fact that the TRAI had changed the yardstick used for measuring DTH numbers and that going by other data, viewership figures for the first three months of 2019 had crossed those of the previous year substantially. The ethical dilemmas and the interplay between information and disinformation that goes viral within minutes has even worried Tim Berners-Lee, the inventor of the World Wide Web. He recently noted that he now feels like 'an optimist standing at the top of the hill with a nasty storm blowing in [his] face, hanging on to a fence' (quoted in Solon 2017).

All the world's great inventors and leaders, like Berners-Lee, set out with one dream. In the case of Gandhi, it was swaraj. In the case of Steve Jobs, it was perfect design, and for Zuckerberg, it was perfect connectivity. In the case of India's current dominant political party, the BJP, it is *akhand Hindu rashtra* (united Hindu nation). And one question all of them initially ask is this: How do I achieve it?

Berners-Lee points here to the other, equally significant questions regarding the ethics and means of using an invention that was articulated a century ago in India by Gandhi: Is it ethically right to want swaraj only because I want it? How can I ensure that the strategy to achieve this target remains ethically justifiable against the timeless standards of Truth (*satya*) and non-violence (*ahimsa*)? Today, many of the new media's master programmers, and its commercial and political users appear to be cast in the mould of ascetics. But most have yet to raise the Gandhian follow-up questions: Why? Why this format? Why push a reductionist version of language, media and nationalism for a multicultural, multilingual nation like India?

Driven by the idea of a Hindi-speaking Hindu rashtra, shaped by India's Right in the 1940s and encouraged by the ruling coalition led by the BJP, a large part of the Hindi media has been promoting a vision of India as *Bharat Mata* (depicted as a Hindu mother figure wearing a crown, dressed in red and gold and holding a saffron flag against a map of undivided India) as central to Indian patriotism. It has also, in editorials and articles, been prophesying that one day soon Hindi will be India's national language.

The fears and worries of the non-Hindi states, ignited by such blatant propaganda, have been further strengthened with some important and senior owners and editors from within the Hindi media being nominated by the government to grace the Upper House of Parliament. One of them was handpicked as deputy speaker. Their presence and the plenitude of government advertising that Hindi papers have begun to carry has had a considerable influence on the fortunes of individual dailies and their owners. But it has also repeatedly convinced voters in the Hindi belt that the Hindi media is India's authentic mouthpiece and an apt vehicle for the core political and cultural beliefs of Hindus. The legacy media's idea of the last century, of the identity of its audience as secular and multitudinous, appears nostalgic, irrational and inaccurate to many within India's mediascape today. As the ground begins to shift beneath our democracy and the old-style media, must Hindi media just race ahead gathering revenue and audiences, leaving wider ethical questions to be tackled by others?

MULTI-MEDIA AND OUR GREY REGULATORY LAWS

The Indian media may not be preoccupied with questions of media ethics, but other serious questions will not go away. What about consumers' individual rights? Or the constitutionally guaranteed freedom of expression? What are the guarantees against commercial and political misuse of private data that citizens are increasingly mandated to hand over to lobbies they do not know or see, which in the wrong hands may pollute their minds with fake news and disinformation?

Can even the most perfect information pathways be stopped from herding citizens and using their personal data commercially without their permission? No matter how grand the vision of a mighty India, reducing a nation and its peoples to one format, one database, taking away from them their essential humanity and democratic rights in the name of securing the nation is still not convincingly justified.

Our legislations pertaining to the regulation of new media in India remain thin on the ground. The Indian Telegraph Act, 1885 (amended in 1961 and 2004), still governs the field of mobile telephony in India. And Article 19(1)(A) of the Constitution gives the print media the same right to freedom of speech and expression as citizens. It is not a fundamental right of the media as in the USA. It comes accompanied by Article 19(2), which lays down that the state can make laws to impose reasonable restrictions on these freedoms, in the interests of the 'sovereignty and integrity' of India.

The free press that has played a vital role in India's democratic functioning is regulated by the Press Council of India with the statutory backing of the Press Council Act, 1978. The print media's right to know has been upheld in a number of judgments. In a judgment delivered in March 2015 (*Priya Pillai v. Union of India & Ors*), the Delhi High Court observed that the new information technology has created a global village and thus the government's action of restraining a Greenpeace activist from travelling abroad and sharing her views with British Parliamentarians was a violation of her fundamental right to free speech and expression.

Should the Media be Banned from Conflict Areas?

On 5 August 2019, the Government of India chose to abrogate Article 370 of the Constitution and bifurcated the erstwhile state of Jammu and Kashmir. This was swiftly followed by a total ban on media and internet in the area (*BBC News* 2019). To protest against this ban, the editor of *Kashmir Times* filed a petition at the apex court. Surprisingly, many Hindi papers and TV news channels chose to support the government's blanket ban on media in the state in the name of national security. In the 1990s, the Press Council had strongly defended the media's freedom when Punjab had faced terrorism. But in August 2019, the Press Council chairman, Justice Chandramauli Prasad (retired), supported the home ministry's decision to block some types of news and information, saying, 'No matter how liberal one is … the fact [is] that some news is best not reported' (quoted in Deshmane 2019).

The question has been hotly debated since, but the ban is in place at the time of writing.

Our Laws on Defamation

In September 2019, a young Hindi journalist from Uttar Pradesh posted a video online showing how already malnourished children in a government school in Mirzapur were being served just *rotis* and salt by way of a midday meal, even though they were supposed to be getting a proper meal consisting of lentils and vegetables with rice or rotis. Obviously, this was a case of embezzlement of resources. The video went viral, but the district magistrate said that a print media journalist did not have the right to take videos and post them online. Following this logic, the district police registered a First Information Report (FIR) against the journalist on the charge of deliberately defaming the state government (Dua 2019). This was followed by a media furore and in December 2019, the UP police cleared the journalist of all charges (PTI 2019).

It is obvious that the definition of defamation is in the eye of the political/bureaucratic beholders. Laws against defamation stem from Article 19(2). Civil defamation in India is not statutorily provided for and is dealt with under the law of torts. But of late, the media has been faced with the rising incidence of being slapped with criminal defamation charges. In an age where information within the digital world goes viral in seconds, defamation remains a tricky issue, particularly for vernacular reporters who are short of finances and legal leverage. It is easy for digital portals to retract objectionable news within seconds, but not for print. And while the laws against disinformation for the digital media remain unclear, frequent use of criminal defamation laws against the print and threats of stringent punishment and prolonged litigation have, on occasion, resulted in undemocratic censorship and the freezing of dissident voices. The case from Mirzapur shows it clearly.

POST-CONVERGENCE NEED FOR TWEAKING LAWS

The increasing convergence of telecommunications and media is a process that has made several older laws redundant. In 2013, the Parliamentary Standing Committee on Information Technology had recommended a single regulatory body for both print and electronic media, or that a body like the Press Council of India be created to monitor the electronic media (see PCI 2012; PTI 2015).

The world of new media is now surrounded by intermediaries: companies that use digital data and information to provide multimedia and related media services. Many of the major intermediary companies are located outside India and are more in breach than in compliance of our cyber laws. Section 2(1)(w) of the Information Technology Act, 2000, defines an 'intermediary' in broad terms, as a person or persons who, on behalf of another party, receives, stores and transmits records as required. The list, as it operates, includes among others, telecom and network service providers, search engines, and web hosting services. They are used extensively by the print and digital media. Today, a large number of intermediaries have emerged as strong media companies, and proper regulation of their activities and definition of the extent of their liability for the information and data they provide the media with is necessary.

THE ELECTION COMMISSION, THE MEDIA AND THE STATUS OF INTERMEDIARIES

The 2019 elections revealed that there is an urgent need to revamp the legal framework regulating today's media. Interestingly, four subjects found mention in the political parties' submissions on the eve of the 2019 elections for reforms in media regulatory laws:

1. The phenomenon of paid news.
2. The threats posed by fake news.
3. Pervasive campaigning via social media.

4. Continued TV telecasts featuring interviews with political
    leaders during the mandatory 'silent period'.

In 2018, a year before the general elections in India, the ECI set
up a special committee to 'initiate a multi stake-holder engagement
process to take stock of the critical gaps in the extant Section of
the RPA [Representation of the People Act], 1951' and also to
'examine the challenges in its implementation and suggest suitable
measures' (ECI 2019: 7). The crucial Section 126 of the RPA that
enforces a 'silent period' (for the 48 hours) preceding the actual
voting, when all campaigning is supposed to cease, was also to be
carefully assessed.

The committee noted that in the two decades following the
amendment in the RPA, the media and the intermediaries that
played a major role in the storage and dissemination of news and
information had grown beyond the available legal provisions for
regulation. The new technologies had introduced new challenges
in the shape of privately owned 24/7 news channels being beamed
nationwide through cable or dish. The three major areas identified
by the committee (ibid.: 15–16) where violations of Section 126 of
the RPA were possible, and needed to be tackled swiftly, were:

1. Live TV coverage of political rallies and speeches during the
    mandatory silent period.
2. 'Systematic and organised' use of social media platforms to
    'manipulate and deceive ... and undermine electoral verdicts'.
3. The fact that the 1996 amendments applied only to the electronic
    media (television, cinematograph or similar apparatus), not
    print, or the electronic media and the intermediaries.

During the process of consultation, the committee invited, along
with all political parties, views from the Internet and Mobile
Association of India (IAMAI) and intermediaries from social
media platforms like Facebook, WhatsApp, Twitter and Google.
While the stakeholders agreed with the ECI that print and digital
media needed to be covered under Section 126, a representative of
the News Broadcasters Association suggested that 'electronic and
digital media' be clearly redefined to include the rights, duties and
responsibilities of all websites, web channels, blogs and vlogs, and

that provisions of Section 126 be made uniformly applicable to all sections of the Indian media and the intermediaries (ibid.: 18).

The representative from the Ministry of Electronics and Information Technology submitted that the intermediaries were only providers of content to be uploaded by print or electronic media. They remained governed by the IT Act, not Section 126. The IT Act provided them immunity on the condition that they issued rules and regulations for users and took down content proven to be violative of laws in force. In view of this, they suggested that the ECI would be better served by issuing advisories to political parties and candidates (ibid.: 18–19). Short on time, ultimately the ECI committee report seems to have accepted the voluntary code of ethics issued by the IAMAI president.

As for the inclusion of print media within the prohibitions of Section 126, except for the BJP, all political parties agreed that it should be done. The suggestion was then duly included in the final recommendations of the committee. The RPA needs to be amended to operationalise these recommendations, but still awaits parliamentary clearance.

The report of the committee was submitted to the ECI in January 2019. But like the Press Council of India's 2010 report on paid news, its contents were brought to the public domain only in July 2019, after Hyderabad-based independent researcher and analyst Srinivas Kodali managed to obtain it from the government's archives by filing an RTI query. By then, the elections had been held, the results announced and the new government had taken charge. By the time the report was handed to the ECI with its recommendations listing new measures for preventing the misuse of traditional and new media during elections, the ECI had a very small window of time left to enforce it. Still, the report is essential reading for those who wish to understand what the mutually dependent future of the media and our democracy will be like in the coming years.

In April 2019, a month before the voting began, a statement was issued by a number of civil society organisations, including two former chief election commissioners of India, questioning the ECI's handling of unaccounted mass campaigning and misinformation being spread via social media and the lack of transparency in its handling of the committee's suggestions (Dasgupta and Guha

Thakurta 2019). It appealed to all political parties to speak up against the use of monetary power in elections and to enact a law to cap the media expenditure of all political players. But the much-required regulation of online content and a cohesive and coordinated framework to regulate intermediaries is yet to arrive.

Larger Ethical Questions on Media Companies Trying to Clean Up News

Since 2014, Hindi newspapers have increasingly retrenched their staff to cut down on expenses and relied heavily on content from various automated platforms operated by digital systems for sourcing news. But most editorials in Hindi have yet to understand how these platforms actually operate, and why and how the stories they are lifting for free 24/7 are being created and uploaded. Intermediaries are becoming powerful sources of Hindi news. News aggregators collect or link articles from various sources into a single feed for users after trawling through thousands of news items (text, videos and images), and then select articles to promote in English, Hindi, and various regional languages.

In a study by the Reuters Institute for the Study of Journalism (Aneez et al. 2019), most internet users in India named search engines as their main source of news online. Of the respondents, 45 per cent said they trusted the news they received in their daily newsfeed, whereas just 36 per cent trusted news overall.

This is the big question today: How does one decipher, in Hindi news, what is real and what is fake? News flow continues through the day and breaking news stories surface each hour. The media needs firm structures in place for quick and thorough news verification, locating and eliminating fake news and stonewalling dubious sources. But in most Hindi news, structures are still somewhat wobbly and the boards of the parent companies are often full of venture capitalists, bankers and advertising executives, many of whom may have their own agendas and may not be too interested in editorial structures, only editorial control. If the editors' authority is diluted greatly, how do printed newspapers, their e-versions and digital news sites find, as the magnificent print line from *The New York Times* says, 'all the news that's fit to print'?

Some Startling Examples of Fake News

In a statement made in February 2019 (quoted by Indian fact-checking site *Alt News*), Facebook India's new partnership head, Manish Khanduri, said, 'We are committed to fighting the spread of fake news on Facebook, especially ahead of the 2019 General Election campaign season' (Chaudhuri and Jha 2019). *Alt News* further reported that the tech giant had added five Indian partners to its network of fact-checkers in India, bringing up their total strength to seven. The aim was healthy: to verify the authenticity of information being fed into it via third party partners so insertion and spread of fake and misleading news could be checked at the source. *Alt News* found that three of these, including one of the most popular Hindi dailies in India, had themselves erred. Their TV channels or print versions had carried false or misleading news, or morphed photos or old videos about a recent attack on a Central Reserve Police Force contingent in Pulwama and a supposedly retaliatory attack on Balakot in Pakistan by the Indian Air Force. Even after it was pointed out to them, most either failed to remove the misleading information in question or issue a clarification. There were also several morphed videos that spread fake news about Islamic nations.

Just before the 2014 general elections, a story by a maverick French journalist was widely circulated (see Sinha 2017). It said that the author had chanced upon a tin trunk containing prophesies by the famous astrologer Nostradamus. One of these supposedly predicted the rise of a star politician, Narendus. The story, once printed in one of India's largest selling English dailies, and then reproduced in Hindi dailies, was never denied or pulled. Among the top 10 most circulated fake news items every year, many are seen to be largely targeting minorities and personalities from rival political groups (see, for example, Jawed 2018).

Consumer resistance could be useful here, but the consumers of news in India are mostly (nearly 80 per cent of our population) below 40 years of age. Most, upon research and during interactive sessions online, display poor communication and language skills, and prefer visiting popular social media sites to flaunt their looks, collect 'likes' and attract some sort of brief 'celebrity-hood'. When they do read print, they do so only to acquire specific information related to jobs or when preparing for various entry-level or civil services exams. When all is said and done, the core competencies of the multi-media industry in Hindi are still largely situated within and linked to the mainstream print media outfits. But one thing is sure, from India's remotest villages to its maximum cities, the new information platforms have totally changed the meaning of social interaction, and age-old perceptions about socio-political discourse and structures.

Since their arrival 15–20 years ago, the deep penetration of smartphones and cheap service providers are pushing Hindi e-papers and news portals that don't have enough well-researched data to reinvent the scene from the ground up the best they can. At the central desks, the machines deployed in journalism make the craft easier. But much remains to be done at the editorial level.

The Hindi media now needs to accept that the web itself is a series of paths and pipes for raw data. It may have been initially designed to be objective, and to drive readers towards verified and truthful stories as opposed to bogus ones, but the business models are largely ad revenue-driven. And ads are driven by how much traffic a particular platform has. Given that stimulating emotions and even confirming biases are proving to be major traffic pullers, the paths and pipes through which the web sends out content are being polluted by aggregators and algorithms propagating this particular incendiary mix as news.

The Capping of FDI for Foreign Intermediaries

Our digital media associations have welcomed the government's 2019 foreign direct investment (FDI) policy aimed at providing a level playing field for Indian news publishers and aggregators. Several news aggregators in India have acquired a larger reach than Indian news publishers and are the beneficiaries of large foreign investments, particularly from China. Since they compete directly with local aggregators and national publishers, the government has decided to cap FDI at 26 per cent. Bharat Gupta, the CEO of the digital wing of Hindi media group, Jagran, welcomed the step as one that will help Indian aggregators produce factual, credible and original content, and shore up credibility among multi-media users in the Tier 2 and Tier 3 companies that non-Indian aggregators are targeting (*Jagran English* 2019).

In a bid to stem the tide of fake news, Facebook has begun using algorithms and user flags to alert users to fake news and questionable stories on the internet. It is simultaneously also posting links to users that can correct the information. On occasion, it also blocks items by sending pop-ups to users. Google too says it has been working to clean up fake news. It has launched measures to make its stories more truth-friendly and actively promotes fact-checking sites so that consumers notice them and news traffic is diverted to such sites. It is also holding workshops for journalists to apprise them of the various dimensions of fake news and how to approach fact-checking sites. Similarly, YouTube is also seized of the urgency of rooting out disinformation. Its spokesperson has gone on record to say that after receiving multiple adverse reports about fake videos on vital matters like health and global warming, they have made several changes to their platform to ensure that such videos are deleted as soon as they are reported (PTI 2019b).

At Microsoft, back to being the world's most valuable listed company (as of 2018), the turnaround, we are told, has been achieved by a realisation that in the long run, rapaciousness does not pay. This has led to a change in priorities. The aim is no longer to chase the golden goose of Windows, but to focus on social networks and smartphones. It is also better to work with regulators instead of trying to outwit or overwhelm them.

The rat race between misinformation or fake news and information is on, and misinformation is acquiring new patterns even as this is being written. But the giants in the media field have at least begun trying to clean up their act. Will we see a digital Geneva Convention for world media in our lifetime? The answer is unclear, but what is clear is that the world has woken up to the menace of disinformation and fake news, and fake news will never have the media field all to itself again.

CONCLUSION

Access to the same technologies, we have realised by now, does not create a similar media globally. The state and the society that the media operates in shape it decisively. Around 2005, it was expected that the mobile phone, when connected to the internet, will prove to be a major disruptor of culturally and politically regressive and undemocratic practices. This has not quite happened. It has penetrated right into the rural heart of India, riding on various regional languages, but with the widening of the public sphere for news and information, major global media giants have entered the scene as intermediaries. Algorithmically driven data is providing important insights into consumer behaviour and much of the editorial power to make decisions is shifting within the media systems from humans to algorithms.

Hindi media today has thus changed and is branching out in ways unthinkable at the turn of the century. But whatever branch of media one is working with, at the end of the day, we all want to keep pace with the mediascape and not fear what we do not understand. Master programmer and virtual reality pioneer Jaron Lanier (2010) was one of the first to predict the changes new technology would bring into information systems, and ultimately revolutionise both global commerce and culture. But he underscored also that information systems need to have information in order to run, and since no information can represent reality totally, there can be no perfect computer analogue for what we call a human being.

The idea that human beings are more than the sum of their available databases should be central to all media planning in any language. But in 2019, the numerically proliferating Hindi media and most of its new consumers are still confused about the world of multi-media. They realise, of course, that when ads are being released, having a million followers on Twitter or Facebook is not the same for a paper as having a million readers certified by the Audit Bureau of Circulations. But what they are often not alert to is the fact that algorithms that drive the digital news that they access with such ease (often for free) may be tracking their personal lives more closely than they'd like and selling the information commercially without their consent. Today, no software is neutral. Hindi's digitised news can and does embed political ideologies and promotes certain consumership patterns. These ideological and commercial biases remain invisible even as they become ubiquitous. Hindi media professionals have to, therefore, be attentive to the news content they are increasingly being 'locked into'.

THE ROLE OF MEDIA REGULATORY BODIES

The other slippery slope is that of present-day media regulations and the state, and operative procedures followed by various regulatory bodies. If the media is indeed free, should governments get to decide how they access, curate and upload content, on occasion leading to governmental overreach? Yet another dilemma stems from the inordinate effect Facebook and Twitter have on Hindi media and its young consumers. It is interesting to see how the vernacular media is facing these various challenges. Traditionally, India's English-speaking consumers, though numerically smaller, have always had better internet products for everything: news, jobs, classifieds, e-commerce, education and finance. In 2018, two young IIT alumni reportedly raised an unspecified amount from a venture capital firm and launched Lokal, an app that works as a platform for delivering local news, classifieds and information in Telugu. It is already said to have one million active users.

How does the media, in particular the Hindi media, propose to deal with the ethical questions that arise from their meek acceptance of covert governmental guidance of their content and embedded journalists who take their orders directly from their political mentors? As the economy goes through a downturn and revenues begin to shrink, will the bad money finally drive out the good? Should the media serve power or the Truth? One thing that might help both India and the Hindi media as a whole is to downplay the segregationist hysteria regarding terrorism and illegal immigrants. It may give a handful of pious-sounding fanatics too great a say in deciding our future. Truth and power cannot keep each other company for too long. If the media wants to follow the Truth, it must go a separate way towards inclusivity and fiscal austerity, as Gandhi did.

8

Postscript

Post-Covid Media

The Government of India's sudden stay-at-home directive at the end of March 2020 to fight the Covid-19 pandemic triggered a two-month nationwide lockdown (Gettleman and Schultz 2020; Hebbar 2020). While the media and its ardent followers complained about being denied their favourite papers at their doorstep, a surprising spin-off began to surface. Within a month, the internet had suddenly risen to be India's main platform for disseminating news and views, even as the print shrank. Slowly, Indians discovered that they could access news digitally in all Indian languages through the internet from within their homes. And it was almost free. The digital format also presented their school-deprived children and publicity-starved politicians with multiple forums and apps as viable multi-language alternatives to expensive public rallies, and campus-based teaching and coaching classes.

Indians' readership of the vernaculars has largely comprised of freebie junkies, to whom brand names or the media's moral obligations towards its readers matter little. Data released in April 2020 by Nielsen and the Broadcast Audience Research Council on the proportion of men and women above 12 years accessing the internet reveals that every other city dweller is now using the internet, with usage being up 54 per cent across cities. In rural areas, thanks largely to smartphones, internet penetration was found to be 32 per cent. The national average is thus 40 per cent, and average viewing time is at least four hours per day. And tellingly, the number of women accessing the internet stands at 35 per cent and men at 65 per cent. Of these, 18 per cent use the internet for chatting, 15 per cent for social networking, 15 per cent for video streaming and 11 per cent for gaming.

The politicians and their media cells saw the importance of courting these audiences within their homes, with lofty *jumlas* (casual quips) and live-streamed scenes of air force planes scattering a million rose petals from clear blue skies to laud 'Covid warriors' (PTI 2020) and popular film stars and cricketers affirming our national resolve to fight the virus as proud Indians (see also *Scroll.in* 2020). Life matters more, and therefore civil liberties and labour laws must, if need be, be sacrificed to save lives: *Jaan hai to jahaan hai!*—If we live, the world lives! And as erstwhile importers of our goods raise tariff walls and, as expected, foreign investments dry up, self-sufficiency (*aatmanirbharta*) is projected as a big, hairy goal.

As the world reels under the pandemic, ethical questions pertaining to our media—about format, and securing accessibility for the poor, just as for the broadband-connected 10 per cent—recede. So, the questions media observers raised as the year 2020 began were: How do we bridge the widening digital gap between rural and small-town internet news consumers and the mostly urban Indians who use 3G or 4G mobiles to link up with the internet? The privacy question too is waived casually to launch the Aarogya Setu app, mandatory for all.

Revenue Models in the Post-Covid Era

Even after the lockdown, public access to the internet will have definitely increased for two reasons. One, because more people will have become adept at pursuing news digitally through free-to-access websites and inexpensive apps, and two, because the new avenues for distance learning for students that digital media has introduced are full of promise. There is also a third reason: the new economy by its very nature will demand that media personnel everywhere enter a lifelong learning trajectory, to cope with the new technological challenges. Turning away from the digital means turning away from the age of 24/7 news.

Now, digital newsrooms need big money for news gathering and even more for the constant upgradation of technology required to remain more user friendly than their multiple competitors. The question arises: What is the ideal model for the digital news world to raise vital revenues? In the West, the *New York Times* and the *Wall Street Journal* have created sound models for themselves that consist of a healthy mix of subscription-based revenue and advertising that includes direct sale deals, branded content created for niche groups of advertisers and programmatic advertising.

But this model cannot be replicated in India. The earlier model, where traffic was driven using paywall-free content, brings big viewership but no money. Then, the two global giants, Facebook and (Facebook-owned) WhatsApp, get 70–80 per cent of the digital advertising in India. Even multi-language apps like TikTok, the new kids on the revenue aggregation block, are by now accruing more revenue than many sober news providers. According to the Alexa rankings, most Indian viewers prefer to visit established news networks. This leaves very little in the market for spirited independent news media groups like *Scroll.in* and *The Wire*. Their launch of subscription-based models saw little progress and may now wither further as the post-Covid economy atrophies the markets.

Another worrisome feature has surfaced: fake advertisements. Google, Facebook and Twitter are all faced with this problem, wherein opportunistic operators are leveraging the fear and panic arising out of the pandemic and violating company policies to issue false, sneaky and misleading ads. In 2019 alone, Google blocked and removed several million dubious advertisements. Figures released in the first week of May note that they also suspended a million accounts for violating the company's policies. Research conducted by all media giants indicates that as the pandemic spreads, this problem will grow unless strictly filtered out (Salve 2020). So they have started acting tough on the guilty parties. Facebook and Instagram have upgraded their filters to ban ads that sell face masks, hand sanitisers, disinfecting wipes and Covid testing kits to ward off inflation of prices and predatory trade practices.

GOVERNMENT'S NEW AD POLICY: WILL IT HELP OR CONTROL THE MEDIA?

The Government of India's Bureau of Outreach and Communication (BOC) in the Ministry of Information and Broadcasting is becoming an increasingly important nodal body for the media today. On behalf of all client ministries, it functions as the sole channel for various paid outreach campaigns covering the print, electronic, outdoor, and social media and websites.

A new print media advertising policy will become effective from 1 August 2020 (*The Times of India* 2020). Under the policy, in the first quarter of the financial year, all ministries will hand 80 per cent of funds earmarked for advertising various programmes and policies to the BOC. This will also cover all the departments and organisations linked to them. So, the BOC will now handle over three quarters of all pay-outs for advertising with media organisations. This policy will have important repercussions for the vernacular media, including Hindi. It will ensure that 80 per cent of the advertising space that ministries buy in the print media belongs to the vernacular dailies. The new policy has further laid down guidelines under which some tribal and under-represented languages, such as Bodo, Dogri, Garhwali, Maithili, Konkani, etc., will be able to claim due attention through a set of new and more relaxed empanelment norms. It is impossible not to see the bounty it offers to the print media in today's ad-starved ecosystem. That it will expect media organisations to be 'favourably disposed' towards any requests from governmental quarters is almost a given.

Almost on the heels of this, the Ayodhya district administration has released a list of nine dos and don'ts for the media, in particular, TV news channels (Seth 2020). According to this list, prior to being permitted to shoot the event live, each channel must promise to keep within a tight format for coverage of the *bhumi poojan* (Hindu ritual to sanctify ground before construction) in Ayodhya, scheduled for 5 August 2020. On this occasion, the prime minister will formally inaugurate the construction of the Ram temple. The plot, after long and bitter litigation, was finally awarded by the Supreme Court to a trust to be formed by the government to erect the temple (M. *Siddiq v. Mahant Suresh Das & Ors* 2019).

The district administrator's order forbids any provocative writing or discussion vis-à-vis the programme for that entire week. It also notes that the owners of the media bodies will be held personally responsible for maintaining law and order during that crucial period. The order also tells channels that during the debates that will follow the event, no disputed views by people opposed to the temple (*vivadit pakshakar*) will be permitted. The deputy director, information, told *The Indian Express*, '[The] media would have no problem covering the event.... [T]o maintain law and order and considering Covid, news channels would have to take prior permission and ensure ... there are no controversial statements and that proper protocol is maintained' (Seth 2020).

Thus, the carrot and the stick.

JIO AND THE DAWN OF A NEW DIGITAL MEGA-COMPANY IN INDIA

At this point, other interesting things have begun to happen in the Indian market. A little before Covid-19 afflicted Indian businesses, Reliance Industries had rolled out an early version of JioMart (in December 2019). Jio Platforms, officially a subsidiary of the Ambani-owned Reliance India Group, has since quietly shed the word 'Reliance', but has been steadily growing as a huge pan-Indian tech platform for all kinds of businesses. Its stated vision is to create a digital hub for 1.3 billion Indians, which all kinds of businesses, the new media and farmers can access and operate from.

Given India's huge markets and the vast number of consumers (Jio brings to the table its network of 387 million connections), Jio is perceived by major tech investors as a world-class digital platform. It is powered by leading tech, broadband connectivity, smart devices, cloud and edge computing, big data analytics, artificial intelligence, augmented and mixed reality, and blockchain. New partnerships have expanded and in April 2020, Jio made a $5.7 billion deal with Facebook in lieu of a minority (9.99 per cent) stake (Das Gupta, et al. 2020). This has lengthened the platform's runway and ensured that the synergy between Facebook and its little brother WhatsApp will not only revolutionise the world of digital media users, but also turbocharge business for millions of small *kirana* shops (small retail shops) that are also hanging on to the same platform.

In May 2020, Silver Lake, a private equity firm that backs tech companies like Skype, Twitter, Dell and Airbnb, announced it will buy a 1.15 per cent stake in Jio for Rs 5,655 crore (*Moneycontrol* 2020). US-headquartered investment firm Vista also decided to pick up a 2.32 per cent stake and invest Rs 11,367 crore in Reliance's Jio platform (Zachariah 2020). Vista is the world's largest exclusively tech-focused fund. It invests in both tech and software companies.

Post-Covid, the Jio ecosystem will not only be India's biggest virtual platform for the new media, but will also handle payments, content, distribution, currency, and of course, commerce for them. By aligning with Jio, Facebook, which was shunned by China, has acquired a powerful local ally and monetisation options, boosting its own midterm future. And with money pouring in after the Facebook-Jio tie-up, Jio may soon emerge as a home-grown digital giant that houses the vital digital triad of networks, devices and content in India.

Things are thus changing incredibly fast in the world of media today. Even as this author closes this chapter, it is quite possible that major technological changes, mergers and innovations will surface. One must therefore resist the temptation to make predictions about what happens when 'the Wild West of the Internet' (as termed by Zadie Smith [2018: 62]) meets the vernacular hinterlands of our extremely volatile democracy. By the time this book hits the markets, even the most informed guesses might have a rather accidental, haphazard quality to them. One must therefore resist careless and easy moves and just urge readers to watch this space.

Glossary

aatmanirbharta	self-sufficiency
ahimsa	non-violence
anasakti	total detachment
ayah	a term from the British Raj, referring to a native nanny
babu	a term of Farsi origin used by the British to denote native members of clerical staff, now also pejoratively used to refer to government bureaucrats.
bhaiya	literally 'brother'; a term first used as a pejorative in Mumbai, which then spread to other places. Initially, migrants (usually poor) from Hindi-speaking areas, mainly UP and Bihar, used the term to address each other as friends. When they later took to dairying, the word became a synonym for milk sellers in Mumbai
bhakha	the spoken word
Bharat Mata	Mother India, often depicted as a Hindu mother figure wearing a crown, dressed in red and gold, holding a saffron flag against a map of undivided India
bhumi poojan	Hindu ritual to sanctify ground before construction
bindu	a dot
boli	dialect

chaupal	a rural square, where ordinary men, and occasionally women, gather for freewheeling discussions
desi	local or homegrown; from the Sanskrit '*des*', meaning 'country'
devi	goddess
dhaba-wallah	person who runs a wayside eatery
durbar	a king's court, which had clear feudal hierarchies marked out by place, dress and freedom to speak
grameen	rural
Hindi-wallah	people whose first language is Hindi; the suffix was added rather derogatively by the English press to mark them out as a different class of people
jati	caste; more specifically, cultural identity
jodi	pair
johar	a tribal term of greeting in Jharkhand
jugaad	indigenous approaches of getting results through locally and easily available material
jumla	a casual quip
khansama	a word of Persian origin, referring to a native waiter (may sometimes refer to a cook)
kirana shop	small retail shop
kos	a native unit of distance
kuli begar	unpaid physical labour
maan dhan	honorarium
maatra	a mark used in Dev Nagari script to modify the inherent vowel sound in a consonant
mela	rural fair
munshi	clerk
quissa	tale
rashtra	nation
rashtra bhasha	national language
sangathan	organisation

sangh	guild of likeminded members of civil society
sanyuktakshar	conjoined consonants (in Hindi script)
satya	Truth
satyagraha	policy of standing up for the Truth; from Hindi 'satya', meaning Truth, and 'agraha', meaning insistence
shuddh	pure
swaraj	self-rule; from Hindi 'swa', meaning 'our own', and 'raj', meaning 'rule'
vivadit pakshakar	people who dispute a basic contention
zar, zoru aur zamin	gold, women and land
zemindar	landlord

References

'A Virtual Narendra Modi'. 2014. *BBC News*, 7 August. Available at https://www.bbc.com/news/av/business-27939865 (accessed 3 March 2022).

ABC (Audit Bureau of Circulations). 2017. 'Print Media is Growing: 2.37 Crore Copies Added in the Last 10 Years'. Available at http://www.auditbureau.org/news/view/53 (accessed 5 May 2022).

Agarwal, Varun. 2019. 'Nearly 20 Million Viewers Opt Out of DTH Services as Bills Start to Pinch'. *The Hindu BusinessLine*, 1 October.

Allahabadi, Akbar. 2009. *Intikhab-e-kalam: Akbar Allahabadi*, comp. Rauf Parekh. Karachi: Oxford University Press.

Amin, Ruhail. 2018. 'Story in Numbers'. *BW Businessworld*, 5 March.

Amman, Mir. 1804. *Bagh o bahar*. Calcutta.

Anand, Utkarsh. 2014. 'Setback for Ashok Chavan, SC Says EC Can Disqualify Candidate for Paid News'. *The Indian Express*, 5 May.

Aneez, Zeenab, Taberez Ahmed Neyazi, Antonis Kalogeropoulos, and Rasmus Kleis Nielsen. 2019. *India Digital News Report*. Oxford: Reuters Institute for the Study of Journalism.

Arendt, H. 1954. 'Truth and Politics'. In *Between Past and Future: Eight Exercises in Political Thought*, 227–64. London: Penguin Books.

'Article 370: What Happened with Kashmir and Why it Matters'. 2019. *BBC News*, 6 August. Available at https://www.bbc.com/news/world-asia-india-49234708 (accessed 28 March 2022).

Aryan, Aashish. 2021. 'Ad Revenue: Facebook and Google Make More than Top 10 Media Firms Put Together'. *The Indian Express*, 4 December.

Ashraf, Ajaz. 2013. 'The Untold Story of Dalit Journalists'. *The Hoot*, 12 August. Available at http://asu.thehoot.org/media-watch/media-practice/the-untold-story-of-dalit-journalists-6956 (accessed 31 December 2021).

Balaji, J. 2011. '"Paid News" Claims First Political Scalp as EC Disqualifies MLA'. *The Hindu*, 21 October.

Banerji, Ranjona. 2018. 'Cobrapost Exposé Shows Indian Media is Sinking. Now We Can Fight Back or be Drowned for Good'. *Scroll.in*, 27 May. Available at https://scroll.in/article/880384/cobrapost-expose-shows-indian-media-is-sinking-now-we-can-fight-back-or-be-drowned-for-good (accessed 3 March 2022).

Chaudhuri, Pooja, and Priyanka Jha. 2019. '3 Out of Facebook's 7 Fact-Checking Partners Have Shared Misinformation Post-Pulwama'. *Alt News*, 18 March. Available at https://www.altnews.in/3-out-of-facebooks-7-fact-checking-partners-have-shared-misinformation-post-pulwama/ (accessed 28 March 2022).

Committee on Empowerment of Women. 2021. *Fifth Report: Empowerment of Women through Education with Special Reference to "Beti Bachao-Beti Padhao" Scheme*. New Delhi: Lok Sabha Secretariat.

Committee on the Status of Women in India. 1974. *Towards Equality: Report of the Committee on the Status of Women in India*. New Delhi: Ministry of Education and Social Welfare.

Coombes, Thomas. 2017. 'On Bullshit: The Essay That Explains the Era of Fake News'. *Medium*, 3 March. Available at https://medium.com/@the_hope_guy/on-bullshit-the-essay-that-explains-the-era-of-fake-news-a0d9a35ad5ec (accessed 3 March 2022).

Das Gupta, Surajeet, Neha Alawadhi, and Dev Chatterjee. 2020. 'Reliance Jio Connects with Facebook for $5.7-Billion Equity Deal'. *Business Standard*, 23 April.

Dasgupta, Abir, and Paranjoy Guha Thakurta. 2019. 'Election Commission Failed to Curb Fake News Online before 2019 Lok Sabha Polls'. *NewsClick*, 30 July. Available at https://www.newsclick.in/Election-Commission-India-Failed-Curb-Fake-News-Lok-Sabha-2019 (accessed 31 December 2021).

DB Corp. 2019. *Annual Report, 2018–19*. Bhopal: DB Corp.

Deshmane, Akshay. 2019. '"Some News is Best Not Reported": Press Council Chairman Defends Position on Kashmir Communication Blackout'. *HuffPost*, 27 August. Available at https://www.huffpost.com/archive/in/entry/kashmir-article-370-press-freedom_in_5d652716e4b008b1fd2140a5 (accessed 28 March 2022).

Dua, Rohan. 2019. 'UP: Journalist Booked for Recording Video of Schoolchildren Being Served Salt and Roti in Midday Meal'. *The Times of India*, 2 September.

ECI (Election Commission of India). 2019. *Report of the Committee to Examine Section 126 of the Representation of the People Act, 1951 and Other Related Provisions*. New Delhi: ECI.

Gandhi, M. K. 1968 [1928]. *Satyagraha in South Africa*, tr. Valji Govindji Desai. Ahmedabad: Navajivan Publishing House.

———. 1977 [1927]. *An Autobiography or The Story of My Experiments with Truth*, tr. Mahadev Desai. Ahmedabad: Navajivan Publishing House.

———. 2014 [1929]. *Anasakti Yog*. New Delhi: Sasta Sahitya Mandal.

Gandhi, Rajmohan. 2006. *Mohandas: A True Story of a Man, His People, and an Empire*. New Delhi: Penguin Books.

Gettleman, Jeffrey, and Hari Kumar. 2017. 'In India, Another Government Critic is Silenced by Bullets'. *The New York Times*, 6 September.

Gettleman, Jeffrey, and Kai Schultz. 2020. 'Modi Orders 3-Week Total Lockdown for All 1.3 Billion Indians'. *The New York Times*, 24 March.

'Government's New Ad Policy to Help Print Media'. 2020. *The Times of India*, 29 July.

Guha Thakurta, Paranjoy. 2012a. 'India Needs Cross-Media Restrictions'. *The Hoot*, 10 June. Available at http://asu.thehoot.org/media-watch/media-business/india-needs-cross-media-restrictions-6005 (accessed 5 May 2022).

———. 2012b. 'Media Ownership in India: An Overview'. *The Hoot*, 30 June. Available at http://asu.thehoot.org/resources/media-ownership/media-ownership-in-india-an-overview-6048 (accessed 3 March 2022).

Guha, Ramachandra. 2019. 'Ram Guha: How a Colonial-Era Law Used against Gandhi is Now Being Deployed against the BJP's Critics'. *Scroll.in*, 4 August. Available at https://scroll.in/article/932704/ram-guha-how-a-colonial-era-law-used-against-gandhi-is-now-being-deployed-against-the-bjps-critics (accessed 5 May 2022).

Habermas, Jürgen. 1989. *The Structural Transformation of the Public Sphere: An Inquiry into a Category of Bourgeois Society*, trans. Thomas Burger and Fredrick Lawrence. Cambridge, Mass.: Harvard University Press.

Havel, Václav. 1990. 'New Year's Address to the Nation'. Speech. Prague, 1 January. Available at http://old.hrad.cz/president/Havel/speeches/1990/0101_uk.html (accessed 5 May 2022).

Hebbar, Nistula. 2020. 'PM Modi Announces 21-Day Lockdown as COVID-19 Toll Touches 12'. *The Hindu*, 25 March.

IMRB (Indian Market Research Bureau) and ORG (Operations Research Group). 1978. *National Readership Survey*.

Jagran Prakashan. 2018. *Annual Report, 2017–18*.

Jawed, Sam. 2018. '2017's Top Fake News Stories Circulated by the Indian Media'. *The Wire*, 3 January. Available at https://thewire.in/media/2017s-top-fake-news-stories-circulated-by-the-indian-media (accessed 17 May 2022).

Jeffrey, Robin, and Assa Doron. 2013. *Cell Phone Nation: How Mobile Phones Have Revolutionised Business, Politics and Ordinary Life in India*. New Delhi: Hachette.

Jeffrey, Robin. 2000. *India's Newspaper Revolution: Capitalism, Politics and the Indian-Language Press, 1977–1999*. New Delhi: Oxford University Press.

Jha, Lata, and Saumya Tewari. 2019. 'I&B Announces 25% Hike in Print Media Advertisements'. *Mint*, 8 January.

Joseph, Ammu. 2000. *Women in Journalism: Making News*. New Delhi: Konark Publishers.

Kapuściński, Ryszard. 1985. 'Revolution 1: Shah of Shahs', trans. William R. Brand and Katarzyna Mroczkowksa-Brand. *The New Yorker*, 4 March.

Khusro, Amir. 1320. *Khalik bari*.

Kislaya. 2019. 'Jharkhand's BJP Government Promotes "Paid News", Offers Rs 15000 per Report besides Pension to Journalists'. *National Herald*, 19 September.

Kohli-Khandekar, Vanita. 2019a. 'The Good "News" in Newspapers'. *Business Standard*, 8 May.

———. 2019b. 'Media & Entertainment Firms Take a Hit amid Slowing Advertising Spend'. *Business Standard*, 21 August.

KPMG and FICCI (Federation of Indian Chambers of Commerce & Industry). 2017. *Media for the Masses: The Promise Unfolds*. Available at https://assets.kpmg/content/dam/kpmg/in/pdf/2017/04/FICCI-Frames-2017.pdf (accessed 5 May 2022).

KPMG and Google. 2017. *Indian Languages: Defining India's Internet*. Available at https://assets.kpmg/content/dam/kpmg/in/pdf/2017/04/Indian-languages-Defining-Indias-Internet.pdf (accessed 5 May 2022).

Kudva, Roopa, and Madhav Tandon. 2019. 'An E-commerce Blueprint for India's "Next Half Billion"'. *Mint*, 29 August.

Kumar, Raksha. 2019. 'India's Media Can't Speak Truth to Power'. *Foreign Policy*, 2 August. Available at http://www.pulitzercenter.org/newsmatch2018.

Lallulal. 1810. *Premsagar*. Calcutta: Sanscrit Press.

Lanier, Jaron. 2010. *You are Not a Gadget: A Manifesto*. New York: Penguin Books.

M. Siddiq v. Mahant Suresh Das & Ors, CA Nos 10866–10867 of 2010, decided on 9 November 2019 (SC).

Mantri, Geetika. 2019. 'Less Women in Indian Newsrooms, Men Get To Do More "Serious" News: Study Finds'. *The News Minute*, 2 August. Available at https://www.thenewsminute.com/article/less-women-indian-newsrooms-men-get-do-more-serious-news-study-finds-106584 (accessed 31 December 2021).

Mathur, Rajendra. 1992 [1971]. 'Aur ab mehnge akhbaron ka yug'. In *Rajendra Mathur Sanchayan*, Vol. 2, ed. Mohini Mathur, Vishnu Khare and Suryakant Bali, 383–87. Delhi: Vani Prakashan.

——. 1992 [1978]. 'Lilliput desh ke chhote-chhote akhbaar'. In *Rajendra Mathur Sanchayan*, Vol. 2, ed. Mohini Mathur, Vishnu Khare and Suryakant Bali, 388-89. Delhi: Vani Prakashan.

'Media Association DNPA Welcomes 26 Per Cent FDI in Digital News Sector'. 2019. *Jagran English*, 5 September. Available at https://english.jagran.com/business/welcome-step-says-jagran-new-media-ceo-as-digital-media-bodies-hail-26-fdi-cap-10004123 (accessed 28 March 2022).

Micklethwait, John. 2019. 'The Future of News'. Lawrence Dana Pinkham Memorial Lecture. Chennai, 3 May. Available at https://www.asianmedia.org/acj/lawrence-dana-pinkham-memorial-lecture-2019-the-future-of-news-john-micklethwait-editor-in-chief-bloomberg-news/ (accessed 31 December 2021).

Misra, Udit. 2019. 'Explained: 70 Years Ago, Here's How the Constituent Assembly Debated Status of Hindi'. *The Indian Express*, 24 September.

Mitra, Chandan. 2006. 'Economics and Politics of News: Editor's and Owner's Dilemma'. In *Making News: A Handbook of the Media in Contemporary India*, ed. Uday Sahay, 47–53. New Delhi: Oxford University Press.

'Modi Praises India's Discipline during Lockdown, Asks People to Light Lamps on Sunday at 9 p.m.'. 2020. *Scroll.in*, 3 April. Available at https://scroll.in/latest/958076/modi-praises-countrys-discipline-during-lockdown-asks-people-to-light-lamps-on-sunday-at-9-pm (accessed 28 March 2022).

MRUC (Media Research Users Council). 2017. *Indian Readership Survey 2017: Key Trends*.

——. 2019a. *Indian Readership Survey Q1 2019: Topline Findings*.

——. 2019b. *Indian Readership Survey Q2 2019: Topline Findings*.

'NaMo TV: It Came, We Saw, It Conquered (the EC). And Now it's Gone'. *The Wire*, 20 May. Available at https://thewire.in/media/as-polls-draw-to-a-close-namo-tv-slips-off-air (accessed 3 March 2022).

Narayanan, Shalini, and Anand Pradhan. 2016. 'New Media and Social–Political Movements'. In *India Connected: Mapping the Impact of New Media*, eds. Sunetra Sen Narayan and Shalini Narayanan, 106–121. New Delhi: Sage Publications.

Nehru, Jawaharlal. 1936. *An Autobiography*. London: The Bodley Head.

Ninan, Sevanti. 2000. Foreword to *Women in Journalism: Making News*, by Ammu Joseph, ix–xii. New Delhi: Konark Publishers.

——. 2007. *Headlines from the Heartland: Reinventing the Hindi Public Sphere*. New Delhi: Sage Publications.

——. 2019. 'How India's Media Landscape Changed Over Five Years'. *The India Forum*, 7 June. Available at https://www.theindiaforum.in/article/how-indias-media-landscape-changed-over-five-years (accessed 31 December 2021).

Orsini, Francesca. 2002. *The Hindi Public Sphere, 1920–1940: Language and Literature in the Age of Nationalism*. New Delhi: Oxford University Press.

——, ed. 2010. *Before the Divide: Hindi and Urdu Literary Culture*. New Delhi: Orient BlackSwan.

Pande, Manisha. 2014. 'Where Are the Women?'. *Newslaundry*, 5 December. Available at https://www.newslaundry.com/2014/12/05/where-are-the-women (accessed 31 December 2021).

Pande, Mrinal. 2009a. 'Blogspotting in Hindi'. *Mint*, 5 November.

——. 2009b. 'Hindi Media and an Unreal Discourse'. *The Hindu*, 18 November.

Pandey, Uma Shankar. 2016. 'The Internet in India: Crystallizing the Historical Inequalities'. In *India Connected: Mapping the Impact of New Media*, eds. Sunetra Sen Narayan and Shalini Narayanan, 221–36. New Delhi: Sage Publications.

Paradkar, Baburao Vishnu. 1920. Editorial. *Aaj*, 5 September.

PCI (Press Council of India). 2011. *"Paid News": How Corruption in the Indian Media Undermines Democracy*.

——. 2012. 'PCI Resolves for More Powers and Conversion to Media Council of India'. No. PR/2/2012-2013-PCI.

Priya Parameswaran Pillai v. Union of India & Ors, WP (C) No. 774 of 2015, decided on 12 March 2015 (Del. HC).

Press Commission. 1954. *Report of the Press Commission: Part I*. Delhi: Manager of Publications.

PTI. 2015. 'Electronic Media May Soon Come under Press Council Act'. *The Indian Express*, 13 March.

——. 2019a. 'Political Parties are Misusing WhatsApp Ahead of 2019 Elections: Top Executive'. *The Wire*, 7 February. Available at https://thewire.in/tech/whatsapp-misuse-2019-election (accessed 5 May 2022).

——. 2019b. 'Fighting Fake News: YouTube to Show "Information Panels" on News-Related Videos'. *The Economic Times*, 7 March.

——. 2019c. 'UP journalist Pawan Jaiswal gets clean chit in "salt-roti" midday meal video case'. *The Print*, 19 December. Available at https://theprint.

in/india/up-journalist-pawan-jaiswal-gets-clean-chit-in-salt-roti-midday-meal-video-case/337877/ (accessed July 2022).

———. 2020. 'IAF, Navy Helicopters Shower Flower Petals to Honour COVID-19 Warriors in Kerala'. *The Economic Times*, 3 May.

Rai, Piyush. 2019. 'Scribe, Brother Shot Dead in UP's Saharanpur'. *The Times of India*, 18 August.

Ramanujan, A. K. 1993. *Folktales from India: A Selection of Oral Tales from Twenty-Two Languages*. New Delhi: Penguin Books.

Rani, Jeya. 2016. 'The Dalit Voice is Simply Not Heard in the Mainstream Indian Media', trans. Kavitha Muralidharan. *The Wire*, 15 November. Available at https://thewire.in/media/caste-bias-mainstream-media (accessed 31 December 2021).

Registrar of Newspapers for India. 2019. *Press in India, 2017–2018*. New Delhi: Ministry of Information and Broadcasting.

'Reliance Jio–Silver Lake Deal: Key Things You Need to Know About Silver Lake'. 2020. *Moneycontrol*, 5 June. Available at https://www.moneycontrol.com/news/business/reliance-jio-silver-lake-deal-key-things-you-need-to-know-about-silver-lake-5367371.html (accessed 28 March 2022).

Reporters without Borders. 2002. *World Press Freedom Index, 2002*. Available at https://rsf.org/en/index?year=2002 (accessed 31 December 2021).

———. 2018. 'Worldwide Round-up of Journalists Killed, Detained, Held Hostage, or Missing in 2018'. Available at https://rsf.org/sites/default/files/worldwilde_round-up.pdf (accessed 31 December 2021).

———. 2019. *World Press Freedom Index, 2019*. Available at https://rsf.org/en/index?year=2019 (accessed 31 December 2021).

Reporters without Borders, and DataLEADS. 2019a. 'Indicators of Risks to Media Pluralism'. *Media Ownership Monitor India*, 27 May. Available at https://india.mom-rsf.org/en/findings/indicators/ (accessed 31 December 2021).

———. 2019b. 'A Delicate Handshake'. *Media Ownership Monitor India*, 29 May. Available at https://india.mom-rsf.org/en/findings/politicalaffiliations/ (accessed 31 December 2021).

———. 2019c. 'Media'. *Media Ownership Monitor India*, 29 May. Available at https://india.mom-rsf.org/en/media/ (accessed 31 December 2021).

Reuters. 2019. 'Modi Govt Freezes Ads in 3 Indian Newspaper Groups'. *Deccan Herald*, 30 June.

RGCCI (Registrar General and Census Commissioner of India). 1961. *Census of India 1961*.

RGCCI (Registrar General and Census Commissioner of India). 2001. *Census of India 2001*.

———. 2016. *Census of India 2011*.

Sahay, Uday, ed. 2006. *Making News: A Handbook of the Media in Contemporary India*. New Delhi: Oxford University Press.

Saikia, Arunabh. 2018. 'Attack on the Home of "Shillong Times" Editor Patricia Mukhim Revives Debate about Media Freedom'. *Scroll.in*, 18 April. Available at https://scroll.in/article/876139/attack-on-the-house-of-shillong-times-editor-patricia-mukhim-revives-debate-about-media-freedom (accessed 31 December 2021).

Salve, Prachi. 2020. 'Manipulative Fake News on the Rise in India under Lockdown: Study'. *India Spend*, 3 May. Available at https://www.indiaspend.com/manipulative-fake-news-on-the-rise-in-india-under-lockdown-study/ (accessed 28 March 2022).

Sampath, G. 2022. 'India's position on the World Press Freedom Index'. *The Hindu*, 5 May. Available at https://www.thehindu.com/news/national/indias-position-on-the-world-press-freedom-index/article65382354.ece (accessed July 2022).

Sen Narayan, Sunetra, and Shalini Narayanan. 2016. *India Connected: Mapping the Impact of New Media*. New Delhi: Sage Publications.

Seth, Maulshree. 2020. 'Ayodhya Event: Do's and Don'ts for TV Include No "Controversial" Parties'. *The Indian Express*, 29 July.

Shramshakti: Report of the National Commission on Self-Employed Women and Women in the Informal Sector. 1988. New Delhi.

Shridhar, Vijaydutt. 2008. *Bhartiya Patrakarita Kosh*, 2 vols. New Delhi: Vani Prakashan.

———. 2019. 'Patrkar Gandhi aur unki patrakarita'. *Navjivan*, October.

Shukla, Ramchandra. 1972. *Hindi Saahitya ka Itihas*, Vol. 11. Reprint, Varanasi: Nagari Pracharini Sabha.

Singh, Vijay. 2018. *Hawker se Haakim*. New Delhi: Gyan Ganga.

Sinha, Pratik. 2017. 'Fake Nostradamus Passages Invented by Francois Gautier and Published in TOI, Zee News for Modi Publicity'. *Alt News*, 29 March. Available at https://www.altnews.in/fake-nostradamus-passages-invented-francois-gautier-published-toi-zee-news-modi-publicity/ (accessed 28 March 2022).

Smith, Zadie. 2018. *Feel Free*. London: Hamish Hamilton.

Solon, Olivia. 2017. 'Tim Berners-Lee on the Future of the Web: "The System is Failing"'. *The Guardian*, 15 November.

Stark, Ulrike. 2008. *An Empire of Books: The Naval Kishore Press and the Diffusion of the Printed Word in Colonial India*. New Delhi: Permanent

Black.

Subramanian, Nithya. 2019. 'In Charts: India's Newsrooms are Dominated by the Upper Castes—And That Reflects What Media Covers'. *Scroll.in*, 3 August. Available at https://scroll.in/article/932660/in-charts-indias-newsrooms-are-dominated-by-the-upper-castes-and-that-reflects-what-media-covers (accessed 31 December 2021).

'Supreme Court Grants Chhattisgarh Journalist Santosh Yadav Bail after over a Year in Jail'. 2017. *Scroll.in*, 27 February. Available at https://scroll.in/latest/830403/supreme-court-grants-chhattisgarh-journalist-santosh-yadav-bail-after-over-a-year-in-jail (accessed 31 December 2021).

Thussu, Daya Kishan. 2016. Introduction to *India Connected: Mapping the Impact of New Media*, eds. Sumetra Sen Narayan and Shalini Narayanan, vii–ix. New Delhi: Sage Publications.

UNESCO (United Nations Educational, Scientific and Cultural Organisation). 2020. *Director-General's Report on the Safety of Journalists and the Danger of Impunity*. CI-20/COUNCIL.32/4, 27 October.

Verma, Mukut Bihari. 1977. In *Lokraj Varshiki*.

Zachariah, Reeba. 2020. 'US Firm Vista Equity Buys 2.3% Stake in Reliance Jio for $1.5 Billion'. *The Times of India*, 9 May.

Index